Forget They Were Ever Born

A Memoir

Sharon Flanagan-Hyde

Dedication

To Mary Jean

TABLE OF CONTENTS

NOTE ON TERMINOLOGY

"What you call people is how you treat them. If we change
the words, maybe it will be the start of a new attitude
towards people with disabilities."

— Nick Marcellino, brother of Rosa,
the young disability rights activist who inspired
passage of federal legislation in 2010

Fifty years ago, people used the term *mentally retarded* to describe a person who was "slow" and didn't develop in a typical way. A generation earlier, people whispered about *morons*, *idiots*, and *simpletons*, the *feeble-minded* and *imbeciles*. Less than a decade ago, President Barack Obama signed legislation known as Rosa's Law that replaced *mentally retarded* in federal health, education, and labor policy with the term *individual with an intellectual disability*. Today, the U.S. National Institute of Health describes intellectual disability as a subset of developmental disability, which encompasses long-term, severe physical disabilities that appear before age twenty-two.

This memoir spans several generations. For historical accuracy, I mirror the terminology used during each time period even though the words might well cause offense if used in conversation today. I adopt this convention with utmost respect for my sisters and brothers with intellectual and developmental disabilities.

NAMES

In some cases, the names of private individuals have been changed.

ENDNOTES AND SOURCES CONSULTED

Attributions for quotations from other sources are included in the Endnotes; bibliographic information is included in the Sources Consulted.

PREFACE

My cell phone rang on a warm January afternoon in 2019 as I sat eating lunch on a restaurant patio in Phoenix, Arizona. I was in the middle of a conversation and let the call go to voicemail. An hour later, my phone showed three voicemails and puzzling email subject lines from business associates: "Were your ears burning?" and "Did you hear?"

The Arizona Governor's Office had convened a meeting that morning of about forty people — legislators, consumer advocates, state agency officials, health care providers, and health plan administrators — to talk about a tragic event that had hit the news.

A young woman with severe intellectual and developmental disabilities and complex medical problems had been raped at Hacienda HealthCare, the Phoenix intermediate care facility where she lived. Although she required constant, hands-on care and weighed only 112 pounds, no one recognized the many signs that she was pregnant. After hearing her moans, staff saw that she was giving birth. The full-term baby boy was not breathing. A 911 recording captured a nurse's four-minute effort to suction and resuscitate the baby. He survived. The mother and baby were transported to a hospital.

I make my living as a consultant working with nonprofit and government agencies, facilitating systems-level changes in health, human services, and education. Four years earlier, I'd worked with a large group of stakeholders to improve Medicaid services for people with autism spectrum disorder. Many of the people who gathered at the Governor's Office that day knew how I tackled complex assignments. A state official asked about interest in a task force to improve abuse and neglect protections for vulnerable people in Arizona. Heads nodded. She then asked if I should be the facilitator. Again, heads nodded.

I'm always happy to have good work, and I readily agreed to take on the job. But what the group of people at the Capitol could not possibly have known is how this particular project connected with my family, or how carrying out the work would re-open childhood wounds that have taken me decades to heal.

1

A BAD DREAM

A shrill scream slashed through my sleep. Confused and scared, I pulled the cotton blanket over my head, making a tent to hold in the last smidgeon of my dream. I caught one last glimpse of a lake, the brilliant green of spring leaves and a sapphire sky dancing on the rippling water. Then the dream was gone.

I sat up. The glow-in-the-dark alarm clock in the upstairs bedroom that I shared with my brother Tim read 2:30 a.m. I knew I should stay in bed.

It was early summer in 1960: Tim was almost four years old, and I was five. Our father, who we called Papa, had told us we were plenty old enough to wait until morning if we were thirsty or had to use the bathroom.

If I got out of bed, Papa might spank me. I lived in dread of his angry words, of his hand reaching for the wooden paddle emblazoned with the Greek letters of his college fraternity. He kept the paddle handy on a hook in our kitchen. It was his duty to teach me to obey without asking questions, he often said. Sometimes he spanked my bottom with his bare hand, sometimes with his belt, sometimes with the paddle.

It always hurt. When he said that it hurt him more than me, and it was for my own good, I didn't believe him.

The high-pitched shrieks came from downstairs where my sisters, Mary Jean, eighteen months old, and Eileen, six months old, shared a bedroom. Between screams, I could hear my parents talking. Wide awake, I decided to risk being paddled. I shivered as I walked barefoot down the knotty pine stairs. Even in summer, it got chilly at night in our house in Pittsfield, a small city in the Berkshire Hills of western Massachusetts. The sleeveless top of my Swiss-dot baby doll pajamas left me with goosebumps on my arms. Hugging myself to keep warm, I perched on the scratchy upholstery of a living room chair. The pink wall tiles of the bathroom framed Papa's dark hair and thin body. He had dark circles under his eyes. Clutching Mary Jean to his chest, he kneeled on the speckled black-and-white linoleum floor. Mary Jean's arms and legs jerked wildly as she screamed and whipped her head backwards.

"Paul, hold her head!" Mom said, half-whispering and half-yelling, as she squatted and spread a wrinkled bedsheet on the floor. When Mom dressed up for special occasions, Papa called her his wild Irish rose. But tonight, her deep brown hair, curled with a Toni home perm, was a messy circle around her ashen face.

"Keep your voice down," Papa hissed. "You'll wake the other kids."

Papa lay Mary Jean on the sheet and rolled it around her whole body, pinning her in a makeshift straitjacket. He gently lowered her into the bathtub and turned on the cold-water faucet. Mom, barely five feet tall, stood on her tiptoes in front of the sink, reaching for a small brown bottle of medicine on the highest shelf of the cabinet.

"Thank God that we got this from Dr. Porter after Mary Jean's seizure last week," she said. Later in life, I would learn that the brown bottle held phenobarbital, a strong barbiturate.

I walked to the bathroom door and peeked in. Mom and Papa didn't notice me.

As Mary Jean lay in the tub, Papa put a dropperful of medicine in her mouth. I smelled oranges. Mary Jean gasped for air as a wave of water washed over her face. My breath caught, and I clenched my fists in fear. I hated the itchy, sore feeling when I dunked my head swimming at the lake and water went up my nose. Water from the faucet might go into Mary Jean's nose and mouth. She might drown! I took a deep breath. I still smelled oranges. Maybe Mom had spilled the medicine. Should I go into the bathroom and help? But I didn't want Papa to spank me, so I cowered silently in the hallway, scared and confused.

After a while, Mary Jean started to respond to the medicine and stopped screaming.

"I think the seizure is over," Papa said.

He took Mary Jean from the tub, unwrapped the sheet, and gently dried her with a bath towel. Mom sobbed and blew her nose with toilet paper. I ducked into the kitchen as Papa carried Mary Jean into the babies' room. Mom followed, pulling a diaper and pajamas from a basket of unfolded laundry on the floor. I scooted back into the hallway so that I could watch them.

"You're OK. You're OK," Mom chanted softly as she pinned the diaper and wiggled the pajamas onto Mary Jean's limp arms and legs.

Papa went to Eileen, who lay whimpering in her crib on the other side of the small bedroom.

"Go back to sleep, sweetheart," he said, rubbing Eileen's back. "It's OK. Go back to sleep."

As I turned to go back to bed, Papa noticed me. I froze in fear. But he didn't spank me. He hugged me.

"Sharon, you shouldn't be up," he said, his voice kind. I was surprised.

"It's the middle of the night. You're just having a bad dream. This is just a bad dream. Let's get you back to bed," he said, carrying me up the stairs. "Be quiet. Don't wake Tim."

He tenderly pulled the blanket to my chin and kissed my forehead. I still smelled oranges. It took me a long time to fall asleep again.

The next morning at breakfast, I asked, "What's wrong with Mary Jean?"

"It's nothing for you to worry about," Papa said. "Eat your cereal."

"Is she sick?"

"I told you, it's nothing for you to worry about. You ask too many questions!"

The kindness in his voice when he carried me to bed was a distant memory. This was the more familiar Papa who would spank me if I didn't stop talking. My stomach hurt whenever I tried to figure out which Papa was in front of me, and the wrong guess always ended badly. Mom, spooning rice cereal into Mary Jean's mouth and then Eileen's, didn't say a word.

We were a typical baby-boom family. Mom had been a teacher but, like all the mothers on our street, quit her job after she got married. Each weekday morning, Papa went off to his job with a metal lunch pail packed with a baloney or liverwurst sandwich and an apple. He worked as a laboratory technician at General Electric, the biggest company in town. GE was not his dream job.

Papa was born in Akron, Ohio in 1924, the sixth of eleven children. His father, Jim Flanagan, left school to work in the coal mines of central Pennsylvania when he was twelve years old. As a young man, Jim moved to Akron for better opportunities and landed a job at a baking company. When the Wall Street crash came in 1929, Jim and his wife Dora had $1,700 in the bank and a mortgage of about $2,000. They lost everything when the bank failed.

Catholic Charities helped them move to a farmhouse in the countryside east of Akron, where Jim and the older boys grew potatoes, corn, and wheat for the family to eat and sell. Dora kept chickens, preserved vegetables and fruit, and baked eleven loaves of bread at a time to keep the family from going hungry. Eventually they moved to a nearby farm with eighty-six acres of land that Dora's twin brother Steve helped them purchase. Jim traveled to construction jobs throughout northeast Ohio to earn the cash needed to support his family and pay back Steve's loan.

"When Pop went off looking for work, my mother packed him a nice lunch," Papa told me during one of our long drives from western Massachusetts across the New York Thruway to Akron. Every summer we made the trek to see our Ohio relatives. Already a budding family historian, I would capture his stories in a composition notebook with a black-and-white speckled cover.

"Pop would come back with practically his entire lunch uneaten," Papa said. "He'd divvy out the food to all the kids. In the summer, the sandwich would have an odd taste because it had been in the hot lunch pail all day."

He described a kinder man than the stern-faced grandfather I knew, the one who jumped out of shadows to scare little kids. Papa's stories about the pressure he felt as a child to step up and bring in money helped me understand the man and father that he became, shaped by the Great Depression and the muck lands of northeastern Ohio.

"When I was ten, I started working in what they called the swamps. The soil was black as night and perfect for growing vegetables. We'd be out there thinning the seedlings in the spring and cutting lettuce and pulling carrots and beets during harvest time. We cleaned the produce in a huge open shed with long vats of water. The farmer graded people on how fast they worked and the damage they did to the plants. Every third day, he fired the ones who weren't up to snuff. We had to work fast and do things right."

One of Papa's most painful memories involved a family who raised gladiolas.

"There was not enough food for everyone in our house, even after the Depression ended. My older sisters left home to find work. When I was about thirteen, Mom packed a suitcase for me. Pop took me to this place a few miles away. He was going to farm me out to live and work there. The lady talked to Pop while the man showed me all the various kinds of glads. But Pop came and got me from the field with tears in his eyes. He couldn't go through with it. I didn't understand why they wanted to send me away. I thought I wasn't working hard enough, and they didn't want me."

Papa and his brothers and sisters attended a Catholic school in the small town of Mogadore. The Flanagans were one of a few Irish-American families in the parish; most were German-American. Although Papa's mother, Dora, was half-Irish and half-German, her children thought of themselves as Irish. Papa said the German kids called his family mean names like micks and bog-trotters. Papa was not a strong student. Red-inked comments on his school papers stuck with him for life.

"The stupid nun who taught ninth grade said the most idiotic thing I ever heard," he told me when I studied Walt Whitman and e. e. cummings in high school. "She asked what I thought a poem meant, and then told me in front of the whole class that I was wrong. The question was what *I* thought! How could I be wrong?" he fumed.

Despite his dislike of the Catholic nuns, he developed a deep devotion to the Virgin Mary as he was growing up.

"We don't *worship* Mary," he said as he helped me memorize catechism questions and learn to fold my hands properly as I prepared for my first communion when I was seven years old. Being the shortest in my class meant that I'd be the first in line as we walked into the church, so it was important that I master getting my hands exactly right.

"We worship God the Father, our creator; God the Son, who redeemed our sins; and God the Holy Ghost. We *honor* the Virgin Mary," Papa explained. "You must honor your mother and me just as we honor the Virgin."

As a little girl, I had no idea how fundamental this conviction was to his sense of self-worth and how he lived his life. In his understanding, Catholics were required to honor their human parents with unwavering, unquestioning obedience. He believed it was his duty to make his children toe a line that he drew, a line that had no wiggle room for normal mischief and misbehavior. He was much stricter than the fathers of any of our neighbors or even his brothers, and his fury went far beyond the swats to the behind that were common during the 1960s. I was terrified of making him angry.

And yet there was a kindness in Papa. When I was preparing for my first communion, he pulled three tiny ceramic pink angels from a wooden shelf hanging in the dining room. The angels were playing musical instruments touched with gold paint — a horn, a violin, and an accordion.

"The priest at St. Joseph Church in Ohio gave these to you when you were six months old," he said, smiling at the memory. "We took you there on your first visit to the farm and the priest blessed you in the grotto. As you grow up, it's very important that you hold firm to your Catholic faith. It is the only thing you can count on in life."

"What's a grotto?" I asked, disinterested in what he was saying about faith.

"A grotto is an opening in a rock. There used to be a gravel pit near the church. The priest decided it would be a perfect place for a grotto just like the shrine to Our Lady of Lourdes in France."

I'd learned about Lourdes in first grade when I went to Notre Dame School. Our parish church was still being built so I took a city bus to downtown Pittsfield to go to the French-Catholic school. Sister Marie Angelique told us about a very holy fourteen-year-old named Bernadette who saw visions of a lady with a white veil standing on a bed of yellow roses. She held a rosary of pearls and asked Bernadette to pray for the conversion of sinners. One day, the lady told Bernadette to dig a hole in the dirt. Water trickled from the ground and quickly grew into a huge spring. People who were sick or crippled touched the water and were miraculously healed. The lady was the Virgin Mary, Sister said.

"The grotto in Ohio is exactly like the one in France," Papa explained. "They put in steel beams to hold up the rocks and installed a replica of the statue at Lourdes. When I was growing up, I had to go home right after school to do chores, so I couldn't go to the grotto very often. But I loved the times when the nuns walked us over to say the rosary on feast days."

These brief visits anchored the Virgin Mary as a lifelong source of comfort for my father, although his faith did not quell his frequent rages.

When Papa graduated from high school in 1942, World War II was well underway. His two older brothers were serving in Europe and Papa wanted to join the military, too. But the United States faced a serious food shortage.

"Pop hadn't done a lick of work on the farm for several years — he was off working on construction sites — so the government said I had to stay home and support the war effort by growing food," Papa said. "It made me really angry."

His brother Jim was part of the D-Day invasion of Normandy and his brother Bill was shot down over Germany and held captive in a prisoner-of-war camp. In Papa's mind, farming was a second-rate way to fight America's enemies.

But eventually, the need for soldiers and sailors grew so acute that he was drafted in 1945 and given a choice of the Army or Navy. His brother Jim, who was in a truck division in Europe, told him to avoid the infantry at all costs.

"Even though I hated the water and didn't know how to swim, I told them I'd take the Navy," Papa said. He was sworn in near the end of the war and spent eighteen months on ships in the Pacific, working on steam turbines and pumps.

When my brother and I were teenagers, Papa warned us about the perils of what he called the secular world. He said he was very innocent when he went into the Navy and the vulgar banter of his fellow sailors left him with nightmares. Photos in dirty magazines, he claimed, burn themselves into people's brains and cause flashbacks.

After the war, he used the GI Bill to help pay for a bachelor's degree in agriculture from Ohio State University in Columbus. His determination as a ten-year-old to be the fastest and most careful worker in the muck lands grew into a whole-hearted desire to be a farmer. But his plan to go home and modernize operations on the family farm would not come to fruition.

2

BABIES LEFT AND RIGHT

"I'd always loved the name Paul," Mom said, giggling, when I was a little girl and asked how she met my father. "When my friend Kathleen told me that her boyfriend was visiting Boston with a fraternity brother named Paul Flanagan, I was interested before I even met him."

Mom was three years younger than Papa and went straight from Pittsfield High School to Regis College, a Catholic women's college run by nuns near Boston. Mom's cobalt blue eyes sparkled as she told stories of her college days, but that was my only glimpse of the high-spirited woman she once was, except when out-of-town relatives came to visit and she drank too much bourbon.

"It was a beautiful campus on a hill," she said. "I did some wild and crazy things. I loved the excitement of the city, the music, going to the theater, the department stores, the throngs of people on the streets. My roommate Elizabeth and I took a bus into Boston almost every weekend. We had so many adventures that the girls in our corridor would ask us when we got back, 'What happened this time?'"

Her favorite story was the time she had a Saturday afternoon date and asked the young man what she should wear. When he said slacks, she assumed they were going horseback riding. They agreed that he would pick her up by a side door of the main college building.

"It was quite the scandal," she said. "He pulled up on a motorcycle. I was afraid the nuns would see me, so I used the paisley silk scarf I was wearing to cover my face like a kerchief. And off we went, down the long circular driveway past the nuns walking two-by-two saying their rosaries. I kept my head down until we got off campus. We went west on Route 20 and had a ball. I was a free spirit on that motorcycle."

That evening the nun on duty made an announcement at dinner.

"Who was the girl on the motorcycle this afternoon?" she sternly inquired.

The room was silent. The nun raised her voice.

"Our honor code demands honesty!"

The room remained quiet.

"I will be in my office for the next hour," the nun said with agitation. "Our honor code demands the honesty of every girl in this room! Those who know the identity of the girl on the motorcycle *will* come and tell me. Do I make myself clear?"

"No one squealed on me," Mom said. "Some of the girls were up on the roof sunbathing, which we weren't supposed to do, and they all saw me leave, but no one said anything. And of course, I didn't go to see the nun. The last thing I needed was for Mum and Dad to get a call that I went off with a boy on a motorcycle. They'd have sent me to a convent! I'm serious. They were not at all happy that I wanted to keep company with young men."

Mom and Papa hit it off right away. After the blind date, they courted through letters, often writing to each other five or six times each week. By the time Papa took an overnight train from Columbus to visit Mom six months later, they were falling deeply in love. They strolled hand-in-hand through the

Boston Public Gardens and sailed around the pond in a swan boat. When Papa invited Mom to the homecoming football game at Ohio State that fall, Mom knew she'd have to evade her strict mother's disapproval. She waited until her Mum was out of town for the chance to tug on her father's heartstrings, pleading that it would be a terrific college weekend and her last chance to go to a big college football game. He granted his permission.

"He sent me $25, which was a lot of money in those days, and told me to get a new outfit," Mom told me when I was a little girl. "I bought a beautiful bright red wool dress to match the Ohio State scarlet."

During the homecoming dance, Papa pinned Mom with his tiny pearl-studded Theta Kappa Phi pin — they were engaged to be engaged. His frat brothers were so happy that Papa had landed a girl that they grabbed Mom from his arms on the dance floor and deposited her atop a fireplace mantle, popping a bottle of champagne in celebration.

"The train from Columbus to Boston stopped in Pittsfield and Mum and Dad came down to Union Station to say hi to me. I was so excited about telling my parents that Paul had pinned me. When I showed them the pin, Mum just chuckled. When I explained what it meant, she didn't take me seriously. That really hurt my feelings. Dad sniffed that Paul had no means to support me. He said that we shouldn't get married until we'd saved $10,000, which was a completely impossible goal. They expected me to come back to Pittsfield after college, get a teaching job, and live with them forever. That's what a good daughter should do."

Saving that kind of money really did seem impossible. The GI bill did not completely cover Papa's university costs. He worked three, four, and five part-times jobs at a time and carried a full course load, sleeping only a few hours each night. He woke before dawn to make sandwiches for a vending cart and then deliver morning newspapers. He washed dishes in his fraternity's kitchen and served dinners at night. He was stressed, underweight, and often sick. When he went home for a few days during the break before his final semester, his father sat him down for a heart-to-heart talk.

"My father and I both compromised," Papa wrote to Mom. "I'll borrow some money from him. I won't take it outright, but it won't involve interest or a time limit for payment. I didn't realize until we talked that I was hurting his feelings by my independence. Pop actually had tears in his eyes that night. I have always been dogmatic about being independent. I have always been smaller than average and never wanted any help from anyone or anything."

Papa went back to Columbus with an agreement that he'd cut back on his part-time jobs and get more sleep. However, the conversation with his father did not iron out the deeper problems between them. Throughout his years at Ohio State, they'd argued about modernizing the farm. His father still used horses to plow the fields and refused to buy a tractor.

One time, home from college, Papa saw a cow staked out in a field, separated from the others. It was hot, and the cow couldn't get to the water trough. He started leading it to the water when he suddenly felt a fist smash into his cheek.

"Pop had come up silently behind me and hauled off and hit me. The cow had mastitis, an inflammation of its udder, and Pop thought the other cows could catch it through the drinking trough. That's not true. Pop really didn't know anything about cow diseases," said Papa. He described the incident as a snapping point.

"Pop was an angry and frustrated man. He felt ashamed that his children had to work and started drinking when he was away from home at construction sites," he said. The drinking made his father mean. He would hit his wife and the boys.

"After Pop got mad at me about the cow, I told him that if he ever hit Mom or me again, I'd have him locked up. And that was the last time he ever touched me."

Papa repeated this story with pride throughout my childhood. As I grew older, I seethed each time I waited for the punch line. He thought that standing up to his father was the right thing to do, but he hit his own children if we talked back. Hypocrite, I thought, putting the word into a silent sentence that I dared not write down on my fifth-grade vocabulary homework. My father is a hypocrite.

As Papa's doubts grew that he'd be able to return to the farm, he began taking education courses. Perhaps he could put his biology classes to good use as a high school science teacher, he thought. He was late to the game, though, and wasn't able to secure a student-teaching position, which was a prerequisite for an Ohio teaching certificate. Nonetheless, he had high hopes that he'd find a job that would allow him to get married and start a family.

Papa's childhood devotion to the Mother of God continued during his college years, when he turned to Mary in prayer during his struggles with emotional balance. In addition to prayers for his own well-being, he offered up communion at mass every Sunday for his father, who for years had refused to step foot in a church. During the Depression, a priest had offended Jim with a remark about needing charity to make ends meet. Papa asked Mom to join him in saying the rosary every day.

"I think our religion and adherence to it is the most important thing we have in common," he wrote to Mom. "I don't see how people can allow themselves to become involved in mixed marriages. If they would make it a policy to date only Catholics, their worries would never exist."

His distaste for all things non-Catholic showed up in his course work. He wrote to Mom, "I really wound up my philosophy course in fine style. I spent the last two class periods telling the class about the Catholic philosophy. They tried to tear all my arguments apart and at times they almost had me. It finally ended with the instructor and most of the class arguing with me. The fur really flew on several occasions. After the class was over almost every Catholic in the room came up to talk with me. They said I presented a very logical argument. I really enjoyed the whole proceedings. I don't know how it will affect my grade. It isn't a wise policy to completely dialogue with an instructor to prove him wrong. I don't care, though. I had to defend my point of view." His combative mindset would grow stronger over time.

He thought a lot about his future with Mom.

"There are so many things we could do with any place we got to make it much prettier and nicer," he wrote. "I've been saving dimes in a jar and have twenty-four dollars and eighty cents towards a place setting of silver. It is really going to be swell planning a home with you. I know we will have a lot of fun after we're married and have children to play with. We can see the dawn breaking over the horizon, darling. Soon we can set a definite date for the wedding."

After she graduated, Mom got a teaching job in Pittsfield. Papa, still a year from finishing college, landed a job during his summer break with the Pittsfield Parks Department as a playground leader. They spent their free time walking in the woods of Berkshire County, watching and photographing birds. They picked berries near Wahconah Falls in Dalton and wandered through the roses and day lilies at a park, making plans for their wedding.

Papa formalized their engagement with a small diamond ring after he graduated from Ohio State, and they set a wedding date. Mom's mother promptly had a heart attack. They postponed the wedding.

"My father told me to never mention a wedding again," Mom said. "Any talk of my getting married would certainly cause Mum to have another heart attack and it would be my fault."

While they didn't break off the engagement, their future seemed uncertain. Papa submitted applications to a dozen school districts in western Massachusetts and didn't get even a nibble. After muddling through a handful of interviews at local businesses, he found what seemed to be a perfect job opening with a family-run dairy. His interview with the husband-and-wife owners started well but soured when he talked about the potential for expanding the operation using modern techniques like artificial insemination.

"Mr. and Mrs. Foster talked with me for a long time," Papa reminisced years later. "They were breeders, and I knew a lot about dairy husbandry and genetics from my work in college. Mr. Foster had a reputation for being really tough to work for, but I wasn't worried, because I'd just do what I was told."

The Fosters excused themselves for a few minutes and then said he was not a good fit for the position.

The next day, General Electric offered Papa an entry-level job as a laboratory operator. It didn't pay much, and it wasn't in line with his interests or education, but he needed a job. He accepted. That evening, Mrs. Foster called back. She had convinced her husband that they should keep up with the times. The job was his, if he wanted it. The dairy farm job was exactly what he wanted to do, but he'd already said yes to GE. It would be unethical to go back on his word, he believed. That set the stage for a career he hated for the rest of his life.

As soon as Papa had a steady job, Mom defied her parents and moved ahead with plans for a wedding and married life. They used the $40 a week that she earned as a fourth-grade teacher for living expenses and banked the $45 he earned in the GE lab. Mom lived with her parents and Papa rented a small apartment in Pittsfield. Even before the wedding, they bought a mahogany four-poster bed and a dining room table they squeezed into Papa's tiny place.

On a cold, cloudy spring day in 1951, Mom's father walked her down the aisle of St. Joseph's Church on North Street in Pittsfield, the same church where her parents and her mother's parents had been married. Papa took her hand in front of the marble-slab altar with Mary, Joseph, and Jesus looking down from stained-glass windows. Mom wore a white satin dress that highlighted her striking figure. Even in high heels, she was so petite that Papa felt taller than his five-foot-six-inch height. Mom's height mattered to Papa. He called himself the runt of the litter, the smallest among the seven brothers in his family. Papa's sister Margaret — called Midge because she, too, was quite short — was Mom's maid of honor. After the mass and the vows, everyone celebrated at a festive reception before the newlyweds left for a honeymoon in Boston.

A few years earlier, the Pittsfield public school system had changed the rule that women had to resign after getting married, but Mom gave up her job right away. Teaching wasn't her life goal — she was focused on being a mother and homemaker. And Papa was eager to step into his role of husband and provider.

Two months after their wedding, Mom and Papa were jubilant when her doctor's office called and said the rabbit died, a coy expression that meant her pregnancy test was positive. A month later, they were devastated when Mom had a miscarriage. Her failure to carry the pregnancy to term fed deep self-doubt.

"I wasn't sure I knew how to be a good mother," she told me when I was pregnant with my first child. "I didn't have much of a role model. My mother was always off shopping and going to lunch with her girlfriends. She dressed me in dull clothes, and I had a terrible haircut. I was a very lonely child. I didn't have friends and my two younger brothers just played with each other. I really worried about whether I'd be able to do a better job when I had children."

Papa desperately wanted to be a father. He relished any chance he got to cuddle babies and play with his small nieces and nephews in Ohio.

Mom soon conceived a second time. Again, she miscarried. And felt inadequate.

"Papa's sisters and brothers were having babies left and right," she said. "I think they looked down on me because I couldn't give my husband a baby. I wasn't a strong farm woman like they were. They thought I was a stuck-up easterner."

A year after their wedding, still yearning for a successful pregnancy, they bought a small Cape Cod style house on Birch Grove Drive in a new subdivision about two miles from the center of town. They negotiated $500 off the asking price of $11,000 by agreeing to fill in the nail holes and paint the rooms. They planted daffodils in front of the house and violets against the cellar wall. A pair of birch trees in the backyard survived from the original grove.

They had 25 cents after they closed on the house. "The down payment wiped us out," Mom remembered. "We couldn't go grocery shopping until the next pay day."

Mom became pregnant a third time and went into labor at five months. Her father joined Papa in the waiting room at St. Luke's Hospital and they sat together anxiously, knowing it was far too early for the baby to make it. Eventually Dr. Cook, the general practitioner who had cared for Mom since she was a child, came out.

"I'm sorry, Jim," he said, turning away from Papa to address Mom's father. "It was a boy. He was too small and not born alive, so we didn't baptize him. Jean bled a lot and had a small stroke, but she should be fine. This should be her last attempt to have a baby, though."

Papa had always hoped his firstborn would be a son. They'd planned to name him Shaun.

"What do you mean, last attempt?" Papa demanded.

The doctor ignored the question and turned again toward Mom's father.

"She gave me a hard time, too, when I said that enough is enough, a baby is not in the cards. She always was a precocious child," Dr. Cook said, shaking his head and leaving the waiting room. He never spoke directly to Papa.

The drooping in Mom's face from the stroke got better, although it tended to reappear throughout her life when she was tired or stressed. Her resolve to become a mother continued. She made an appointment with an obstetrician, hoping a specialist could help. After a quick examination, the new doctor said that scar tissue from a childhood appendectomy had misaligned her uterus. He recommended surgery.

Once again, Mom's parents tried to steer a major decision. "You've done your duty," her mother told her. "Three tries are enough. Just move to another bedroom and go on with your lives."

Catholic prohibitions against any form of birth control meant that celibacy was the only reliable way to avoid pregnancy. But Mom defied her parents again. She had the surgery and quickly became pregnant a fourth time, with me. I was born in 1955.

When Mom came around from the twilight sleep medication the doctor gave her during the delivery, she was alarmed to see a black-and-blue mark on my cheek. She begged the nurses to tell her what was wrong, but they said she'd have to talk with the doctor. She sobbed for hours. Finally, just before dawn, Dr. Dutton arrived at the hospital and a nurse urged him to talk to Mom. He told her that the discoloration was from the forceps he'd used to pull me out.

"It's not life threatening," he assured her, but the bruise fueled her insecurity.

My baby photos show a euphoric father — he truly enjoyed children too young to talk back to him — and an exhausted mother. Mom tried to breastfeed me but didn't know how. Her mother had bottle-fed her three children.

"Nana told me that breastfeeding was distasteful," Mom said when I was preparing for the birth of my first child. "She made terrible comments that only immigrants — the Polish and the Italians — did such a thing."

Mom quickly gave up her attempt to breastfeed and switched to a bottle, but I still screamed in hunger. Flouting the advice of the experts, Papa started feeding me rice cereal when I was two weeks old. Mom argued, saying that I was much too young for solid food. Papa told her that she worried too much, and he'd been around far more babies than she had. His comments underscored Mom's fears that she would never be up to snuff as a mother.

When I was sixteen months old, my brother Timothy was born. I don't remember a time when he wasn't at my side. We'd stand in the bathroom watching Papa shave each morning, hoping he'd give us a bit of shaving cream to smear on our faces. We played in a sandbox Papa built in the backyard and swam together in front of my grandparents' red-shingled cottage on Pontoosuc Lake, about a fifteen-minute drive from our house. Papa gave us "motor boat" rides in the water, holding our arms and whirling us around as we kicked our legs. Tim and I would sit cross-legged on the living room floor as Mom played *Buttons and Bows* and *You Are My Sunshine* on her small upright piano. We banged spoons against saucepans in a vain attempt to keep beat with the rhythm. But as soon as Papa got home, we quieted down. He didn't like commotion inside the house. He might pull the paddle from the wall if we didn't behave like ladies and gentlemen.

The year I was three, a small suitcase appeared by the front door after Mom and Papa took down the Christmas tree and boxed up the decorations.

"That's for when I have the new baby," Mom told Tim and me. "I'll bring it with me to the hospital and when I come home, you'll have a new little brother or sister."

Every morning Tim and I tripped over each other, scrambling down the stairs from the bedroom we shared to see if the suitcase was still there. Day after day, it sat by the front door and Mom was in the kitchen, ready to pour Cocoa Puffs into a cereal bowl for Tim and Sugar Frosted Flakes for me.

Finally, on a Monday morning, the suitcase was gone. We ran to the kitchen and found a strange woman.

"Where's Mrs. Kent?" I asked, knowing that our next-door neighbor would take care of us if Mom had to go to the hospital during the night.

"Come and gone," the woman answered.

Smoke poured from the toaster as two pieces of burned bread popped up.

"Sit down and eat your breakfast," she said.

"We eat cereal," Tim answered.

"Today you eat toast." She smeared oleomargarine over each piece.

"It's burned," I said.

"Eat it anyway."

The toast tasted terrible.

"We want cereal like my mom gives us," I said.

"You'll both sit there until you finish that toast."

I don't remember what happened next or even the woman's name. Tim and I called her the burned-toast lady. We hated her.

When Papa opened the back door that evening, I ran to him.

"That lady made us eat…"

He cut me off.

"You have a new sister named Mary Jean! Mary after the Virgin Mother, and Jean after your mother. Seven pounds, five ounces!"

He was excited and happy. I missed Mom and wanted to see the new baby, but children weren't allowed at the hospital.

After a week, Papa finally brought Mom and the baby home. Mary Jean's tiny face, round and pink, peeked above a pale green and yellow blanket when Mom bent down to show her to Tim and me. Then Mom put Mary Jean in a little white crib called a bassinet.

Sharon, Tim, and Mary Jean —
House on Birch Grove Drive, Pittsfield, January 1959

"You and Tim slept in this bassinet when you were babies," Mom said. "When Mary Jean gets a little bigger and learns to sit up, she'll sleep in the regular crib, just like you did."

Even though Mom was busy boiling Mary Jean's bottles and washing diapers, I was happy to have her home and even happier to have a baby sister. I loved holding her soft hands and stroking her cheek.

"How long until she's big enough to play with me?" I asked.

"Soon enough," Mom said. "She'll be running around with you and Tim before you know it."

Mary Jean grew big enough sleep in a crib a few months later, but I noticed she was different than other babies in our neighborhood. She didn't smile at people. She had no interest in dolls or stuffed animals. She didn't babble or coo. I talked to her and made funny noises to try to get her attention, but she wouldn't look at me.

When Mary Jean was seven months old, we went to Ohio for a week's vacation. To make the long drive more comfortable, Papa cut a piece of plywood just the right size to cover the back seat of our sedan and extend over the foot space. He tucked the diaper bag and small suitcases in the empty space and put a blanket over the plywood. It was a cozy platform for Tim and me to color, eat snacks, and take naps. Tim and I got restless, but Mary Jean lay placidly in Mom's arms or slept in a corner of the back seat.

Papa's brothers and sisters and their wives and husbands and kids assembled at the farm to spend time with us. Tim and I played with our cousins in the barn and near the stream, listening to the shouts of parents telling us to not go under the stone bridge. A troll lived under the bridge, the older cousins claimed. The bridge was dangerous and might fall on our heads, the uncles said. After hours of play, word spread that it was time to eat. An enormous expanse of food filled the biggest picnic table I'd ever seen, with fried chicken and casseroles and potato and macaroni salads and more kinds of Jell-O salad than I could have imagined.

Babies were passed from lap to lap. Mary Jean was the youngest that summer. Our cousins Debbie, John, and Mike were one-year-olds, and Billy was two. We had twenty Flanagan cousins at that point — Grandma and Grandpa Flanagan eventually had forty-two grandchildren. My cousin Sue, who was ten at the time, vividly remembers that particular picnic. Dora Mae, Sue's mom and Papa's older sister, held Mary Jean for a while and then asked to talk with Papa privately. Years later, Sue told me what she knew about the conversation.

"There's something wrong with Mary Jean," Dora Mae said. "Her muscles are too stiff. She doesn't react to people like a normal baby. You need to take her to the doctor as soon as you get back to Pittsfield and find out what's wrong with her."

Papa exploded with anger. "There's nothing wrong with Mary Jean! She's just fine!"

Mom began crying when Papa told her what Dora Mae had said. Others in the family told Dora Mae she shouldn't have spoken up. Dora Mae was a nurse and had three young children of her own. She was sure that she'd spotted something that needed a doctor's attention but felt terrible about upsetting my parents. She regretted saying anything, Sue told me.

But a few months later, Papa called Dora Mae to apologize. Mary Jean's pediatrician had confirmed that something was amiss — they just weren't sure what it was.

Eileen was born almost exactly a year after Mary Jean. "Four babies in five years," Mom often said, with exhaustion and pride. When Mom worried that Eileen might also be slow, Dr. Porter, our pediatrician, reassured her, but suggested a series of shots just in case. Years later, Papa claimed that Dr. Porter's daughter was doing experiments on whatever the shots contained. I don't know if Eileen was given a drug or a vitamin, or whether Papa's version of the story was accurate.

Mom said she never thought to ask what the shots were —
she just trusted the doctor.

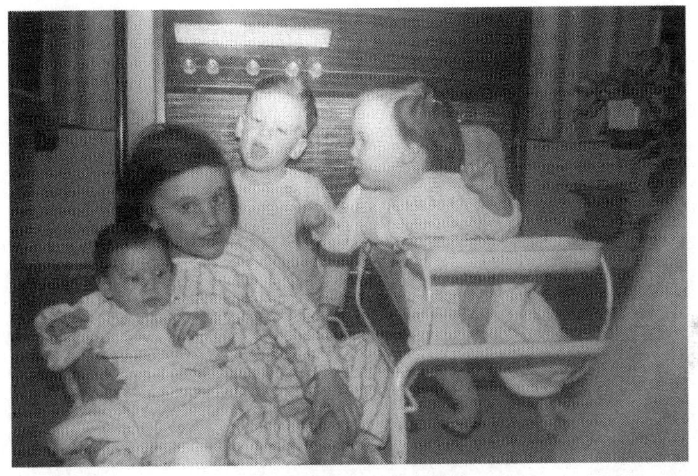

Eileen, Sharon, Tim, and Mary Jean —
House on Birch Grove Drive, Pittsfield, Winter 1960

Eileen was strong. She and Mary Jean shared the tiny
downstairs bedroom, their cribs taking up most of the room.
By spring Eileen smiled and babbled most of the time. She
rolled from her tummy to her back. By summer, she played
happily with toys.

"Eileen is ahead of schedule on all her development
milestones," Mom proudly told the neighbors.

"It's probably because of the shots," Papa added. He never
believed that Eileen's athleticism as a child or her teenage
prowess as a dancer and skier were innate, and praising Eileen
would make Mary Jean's problems even more noticeable.
His reticence to speak about Eileen's accomplishments was a
hallmark of her many struggles to be seen by our parents as
smart and capable. Over the years, Papa often made comments
that eroded my confidence, too. He said that because I was

small for my age, I shouldn't try to hang from the playground monkey bars or learn to hit a softball. It was OK for my brothers to ride their bikes fast and sail boats on Pontoosuc Lake, but it was better for girls to just help out around the house.

Eileen, Sharon, Mary Jean, Tim —
Grandparents' house on Circular Avenue, Pittsfield, 1960

A friend of our grandmother named Adelaide gave Mary Jean and Eileen hand-smocked white nightgowns. Tiny stitches around the neck gathered the fabric in pretty patterns.

"Eileen and Mary Jean look almost like twins," Mom said after she slipped the nightgowns over their heads.

It wasn't really true that they were like twins, I thought at the time. Their hair was the same color and cut the same way, but they didn't seem at all alike to me. This, too, would haunt Eileen. She never felt that she was seen for herself — she was defined as Mary Jean's "twin" sister, only twelve months younger.

Their nightgowns matched, but their development didn't. Eileen stood in her crib, holding on to the railing, jumping up and down, giggling and laughing. Mary Jean sat in the corner of her crib, staring at a rubber doll. She looked at it for a long time, then turned it over, then looked some more. She didn't smile or make noises. It was as if she were asleep with her eyes open.

3
DEVELOPING MORE SLOWLY

The night I witnessed Mary Jean's seizure when I was five years old was the beginning of a profound change in our family, because the seizures continued. My sister screamed for hours at a time, day and night. During the day, Mom walked with Mary Jean in her arms, hour after hour, looping through our small house: kitchen, dining room, living room, hallway, and back to the kitchen, trying to quiet Mary Jean's high-pitched shrieks. When Papa came home, he took over, often walking Mary Jean in the same loop.

It was the summer of 1960, and I was excited about starting kindergarten at Egremont School on the Tuesday after Labor Day. Egremont was about three-quarters of a mile from our house on Birch Grove Drive, down Elm Street and up a small hill. Mom went over the plan with me: I'd walk with a bunch of older kids from our street in the morning and back home with two other kindergarteners at lunchtime.

I was thrilled that Mom and Papa were going to let me walk without a grownup. Mostly I felt like an outsider on our street. Every time neighborhood kids ran from yard to yard, playing tag or hide-and-seek, Tim and I had to find a parent and ask permission to move from one family's yard to another's. By the time we'd rejoin the group, they'd moved on to another yard, and we repeated the whole rigmarole. Finally, walking with other kids to school, I'd be like everyone else.

But I worried about Mom handling my younger siblings while I was at school. I did my best to help with housework, and to keep Tim and Eileen out of trouble, while Mom took care of Mary Jean. I fretted all the time about what was wrong with Mary Jean. A lady on our street told Mom that I seemed like a little old lady, always fussing over things.

All summer long, unless it was raining, Papa would walk with Mary Jean, up and down the sidewalk in front of our house, while Mom made supper. He held Mary Jean against his shoulder as he dodged children on tricycles, hoping she'd stop crying. If she calmed down, he put her feet on the ground, coaxing her to walk. She refused, curling up her legs and clinging to his hands, suspended in the air.

If Mom was particularly tired, Papa took Tim, Eileen, and me with him to Imperial Bowl where his league played once a week. As he parked the car, he'd always remind us to not cause any trouble. It was fun at the alley — the noise of the pin-setting machines and boisterous cheers meant we could be a bit rowdy and Papa wouldn't notice. His teammates teased us about being alley-rats and particularly liked Eileen's cheerful chitchat.

One Saturday morning, Eileen lifted a bowling ball a couple inches off the floor and dropped it on her toe. When she howled in pain, Papa looked annoyed. He continued his turn without checking to see if her toes were broken. Another man on the team took off her shoe, told her to wiggle her toes, and gave her a hug.

On another day, a man on the bowling team offered me half of his Hershey's bar.

"You're pretty scrawny, aren't ya kid," he said as he held it out.

Eager for a rare treat, I smiled and looked toward Papa.

"No," Papa said. "I can feed my family perfectly well."

"But Papa," I whined. "Please?"

"I said no!"

"But…"

"You know how you should behave," he said, his face dark red. "We are the Flanagans."

He spanked me as soon as we got home.

At the end of August, Mom took me shopping for school clothes at Zayres, a huge new department store down the hill from Adams Market on Dalton Avenue. Everything was on one floor — clothes, toys, fabric and sewing patterns, hammers and nails. An enormous escalator connected Zayres with Adams, where we shopped for groceries. Zayres was completely different from Pittsfield's other big department store, England Brothers, which was downtown on North Street and had six floors. England's had escalators between floors and an elevator operated by a man in a uniform with brass buttons. I liked visiting Santa Claus and Robert the Talking Reindeer at England's every year, but Zayres was more exciting. Except for the perfume counter, England's smelled like a musty old house. Zayres' snack counter made the whole store smell like popcorn.

Zayres was the first of the big-box discount stores in the suburbs that would eventually spell the end of iconic department stores like England's and fuel the decline of downtown Pittsfield. But as a child, I loved that Zayres had bright lights and racks of beautiful dresses, jumpers, and blouses. However, as excited as I was with the prospect of new clothes, I was embarrassed to be so small for my age. I'd turned five in March but still wore a size 3T. I knew that the T stood for "toddler." I was not a toddler. It seemed to me that the clothes factories should come up with different sizes for older kids who happened to be short.

I went off to my first day of school in a blue sweater and a new plaid skirt. But after a few weeks, my excitement about fresh crayons and sharp pencils and stacks of pale green paper waned. I was bored. The teacher made us sit up straight at our desks and repeat the first seven letters of the alphabet. Mom had already taught me the whole alphabet. One day, fed up and restless, I started with H instead of A when the teacher led us in a sing-songy group chant. I got as far as K when the teacher told everyone to be quiet.

"Sharon," she said. "Please do as you are told. A-B-C-D-E-F-G."

I put my head down, feeling ashamed and indignant. I wanted her to know that I could say the whole alphabet. I wanted her to teach me how to read. But I was afraid that if I talked back, the teacher would send a note to my parents and I'd get in trouble again for talking too much.

One day, an ear infection and fever kept me home. I settled on the couch to watch Romper Room and Captain Kangaroo on our black-and-white TV. Tim was at Tiny Tots preschool, and Eileen was napping.

"Can I have pancakes?" I asked Mom when she came to check on me after putting Mary Jean in the baby swing in the backyard.

She rarely made pancakes. I liked them with melted oleomargarine and Aunt Jemima syrup drizzled over the top.

"OK, I guess I can do that," she said.

I heard the refrigerator door open and close, and a bowl and spoon clinking in the kitchen.

Mary Jean started screaming in the yard. The back door slammed as Mom went outside. A few minutes later I walked through the hallway to go to the bathroom, and a flickering light in the kitchen caught my eye. School bus yellow reflections bounced off the door of the smudged white refrigerator. It was cloudy outside, so it couldn't be sunlight. I ran into the kitchen.

"Fire," I yelled. "Mom, there's a fire on the stove! Mom, there's a fire!"

Mom had put a saucepan on the stove to melt oleo for my pancakes. Flames shot into the air. Mom left Mary Jean in the swing and raced inside. She dumped salt from a round container on the fire, then slammed a lid on the pan. Black smoke billowed toward the ceiling as the flames disappeared.

Crying, Mom walked past me, back to Mary Jean and the swing. She pushed her, crying and crying, as Mary Jean screamed. I dragged a metal stepstool over to the sink and climbed the two steps. I tried to lean across the sink and reach the kitchen window. My arms weren't long enough, so I kneeled in the sink. The window was hard to move, but I kept at it and finally got it open a few inches. Smoke drifted into the backyard. After a while, Mom and Mary Jean stopped crying. Carrying Mary Jean, Mom came back in the kitchen.

"Any time there's a grease fire," she said, her voice catching, "you need to cut off the oxygen. The salt and the pan lid cut off the air. Never throw water on a grease fire — it could splatter and set your clothes on fire."

I nodded silently as Mom dialed the phone.

"Paul, there was a fire." She was crying as she spoke. "We're OK, but the paint in the kitchen is ruined. I'm sorry. I'm so sorry."

I went to the bathroom to pee. I wasn't hungry any more. I was really sorry that I asked for pancakes.

Papa came home from work early. The walls and ceiling were dirty with smoke.

"What were you thinking?" he yelled at Mom. "Why can't you use your head?"

Mom had used her head when she put out the fire, I thought, but I didn't say anything. Cowering from the intensity of Papa's rage, I managed to keep my mouth shut. Papa mixed Pine-Sol in a bucket of water and scrubbed the ceiling and kitchen walls. The stink of smoke and the pine smell from the soapy water reminded me of campfires near my grandparents' cottage during the summer.

"I'm so sorry, Paul," Mom kept saying. "I'm so sorry. Sometimes Mary Jean calms down when I put her in the swing. I was just trying to get Mary Jean to stop crying. I'm so sorry."

The kitchen was back to normal when it was Mom's turn to host bridge a couple months later. The mothers in our neighborhood played on the second Tuesday of every month, rotating from house to house. The afternoon of the party, I moved toys from the living floor into the hall closet to make room for two folding card tables and chairs that Mom borrowed from Mrs. Allison next door. Mom cleaned the bathroom and told us not to make a mess when we used the toilet and brushed our teeth.

"Do you think there's enough soda?" she said to no one in particular after we ate an early supper. She put the fancy Libbey highball glasses that she'd gotten with S&H green stamps on the dining room table, along with bottles of cola and lime soda. She arranged bowls of pretzels, ashtrays, and decks of cards on each folding table, then moved everything around three or four times.

"Don't be so jittery," Papa said. "I don't know why you make such big deal out of everything."

Papa always wanted the neighbors to admire the snapdragons he planted in front of our house, and hoped the men on his bowling team would notice that his footwork was just right as he approached the lane. He didn't seem to realize that Mom wanted people to think well of her, too.

Mom's mouth got tight, but she didn't say anything. Papa gave Mary Jean phenobarbital even though she wasn't having a seizure. She fell asleep right away, which Papa said was a blessing because he had no interest in listening to a hen party if he had to stay home to keep Mary Jean quiet. He never missed an opportunity to make derogatory comments about women. Papa tucked the rest of us into bed and went bowling, even though it wasn't his normal bowling night.

I heard the front door open and close a few times and the sounds of women talking and laughing. I smelled smoke, which scared me until I realized it was cigarettes. Mom and Papa didn't smoke at home, but I recognized the odor from the Model Dairy on Ontario Street where we sometimes got ice cream cones. I couldn't sleep, so I sat at the top of the stairs and listened. Even though I was very young at the time, I clearly remember the conversation.

"Is Mary Jean doing any better?" Mrs. Mason asked. She lived at the end of our street, on the cul-de-sac by the path to Brattle Brook Farm, so she couldn't hear Mary Jean's screams like our closer neighbors.

"Mary Jean is still developing more slowly than our first two," Mom said. "The doctor says she'll probably catch up." Her voice was wobbly. "At least she never wakes the other children when she's crying at night."

That's not true, I thought. I didn't understand why my parents told Tim and me that we shouldn't lie, but then said things that weren't true. We all woke up at night. Tim and I knew enough to stay in bed. And Eileen, still a toddler, had already learned to not make a fuss if Mary Jean was having an episode. Instead, she'd smile sweetly from her crib, trying to elicit a smile from Mom and Papa.

"Well, you certainly don't want to let things get out of hand," Mrs. Branson said. "There must be things you can do to push her along. She's what — almost two years old now?"

Mrs. Branson lived across the street and had a bunch of kids. Papa called her a know-it-all who got into people's business. I remember her as a woman who expressed her ideas openly, defying the norm that men were in charge and women should defer to their husbands.

"Well, the doctor says that we just have to wait and see," Mom replied in a sad voice.

Sitting there on the top step, I decided that as the oldest, it was my responsibility to take charge of pushing Mary Jean along. The next afternoon after kindergarten, I stayed in the house after lunch instead of going in the backyard to play. Mom turned on the TV to watch her soaps, *As the World Turns* and *Guiding Light*, and propped Mary Jean against a pillow on the living room floor. I sat down, too, and rolled a small red ball with blue and yellow stripes in Mary Jean's direction.

"Ball," I said.

Mary Jean didn't roll the ball back, so I crawled over and put the ball in her hands.

"Ball," I said. "Ball."

She dropped the ball on the carpet. I put it in her hands again. When it slipped from her hand, I put the ball on my head like a hat. Mary Jean ignored me. I hid the ball behind my back and made it pop up over my shoulder. Mary Jean didn't smile, but she said "ba."

"Mom," I yelled. "She said ball! Mary Jean said ball!"

"Good job, Sharon," Mom said. "Another new word!"

At the next commercial, Mom asked me to find her a pencil. The pediatrician had told Mom to keep a list of Mary Jean's words. I stretched to reach the pencil jar near the phone on the kitchen counter. Mom sat at the table and added "ball" to the list.

"Six words," Mom said. "She has six words now."

Mary Jean echoed the words she heard, but she never asked for anything on her own. Eileen was only eight months old, but she babbled all the time and understood words like "cup" and "juice."

In January 1961, Mary Jean turned two and Eileen, one. With birthdays so close together, Papa said it made sense just to have one cake and celebrate on Eileen's actual birthday, since it was a Friday. Mom's parents, Nana and Gramp, said that we should come to their house for dinner. Gramp would pick up a cake at the Pittsfield Rye Bakery so that Mom wouldn't have to trouble herself with baking.

Nana and Gramp lived a few miles from us in a Victorian-style house that Nana's grandfather built in 1884. Because the address was 52 Circular Avenue, everyone in the family — even out-of-town relatives — called the house Fifty-Two. Nana's sister, our great-aunt Eleanor, and Mom's brother, our Uncle John, lived there, too. Jilted as a young woman by a ne'er-do-well fiancé, Aunt El never married. Papa once called her a dried-up old spinster. Uncle John, a lawyer who usually smelled like whiskey, was also single. It seemed strange to me that even though he was grown up — almost thirty years old! — he still lived with his parents.

When we walked into Fifty-Two, Gramp was watching the news. He was in fine fettle. John Fitzgerald Kennedy, the handsome Irish-Catholic senator from Massachusetts, had been inaugurated that day as president of the United States after defeating Richard Nixon. Even though we weren't related, our family claimed Kennedy as one of our own. The black-and-white screen showed Jackie Kennedy, the new first lady, in a coat with big buttons and pockets, long white gloves, a pillbox hat that Mom said was stylish, and a big furry muffler. She stood next to the president — Jack, Gramp called him — who wore a dark tuxedo and top hat.

"Jackie looks stunning," Mom gushed. "An A-line is always so flattering. Who'd even suspect that she has a newborn baby?"

Gramp rolled his eyes.

"Come here, Sherry," he said, gesturing to his lap. He was the only one who called me Sherry, and the only one who thought that, at five years old, I was old enough to understand politics. Throughout the summer and fall, he'd explained the presidential campaign to me.

"Sit here with me and listen to what's really important."

I snuggled with him in his big red leather chair. He put his feet up on the matching ottoman.

"Dwight Eisenhower is heading to retirement, Tricky Dick has his tail between his legs, and Jack Kennedy will lead us to a new frontier," Gramp said. "He's a progressive. That means he's going to get Congress to make a lot of changes that will be good for the common man."

I often watched *Meet the Press* with Gramp when we stopped by Fifty-Two on Sunday mornings after church, so I knew how much he disliked Nixon. He'd told me that Tricky Dick used dirty politics to get elected to the Senate. I felt proud that Gramp didn't treat me like a little kid. He fed my eagerness to learn. He explained the way the government worked in America and how the British oppressors caused his grandparents to flee the famine in Ireland in the 1840s. Papa shook his head when Gramp talked about history and politics, saying I couldn't possibly understand what on earth all these things meant. But I did understand, and I remembered everything that Gramp told me.

While Nana and Mom finished cooking dinner and the babies played on the living room floor, Aunt El, a church organist and piano teacher, told Tim and me to come into the front parlor for a lesson on the baby grand piano that filled up one side of the room. I hated piano lessons. The keys of her piano were harder to press down than Mom's small piano at home. I started at middle C and slowly made my way up the scale. Aunt El was impatient when I used my index finger instead of my middle finger to cross over when I came back down, which meant I ran out of fingers before I got back to middle C. She sighed and said that it was painfully obvious that I hadn't practiced at home. After a few minutes, she asked Tim to play. Grateful to be off the hook, I went back to the living room so I could watch TV with Gramp. We ate dinner quickly, eager for cake. As we sang Happy Birthday, Eileen blew out three candles — one for her and two for Mary Jean, who sat impassively staring at the cake.

After Mary Jean turned two, Papa would take her outside after work, determined that she learn to walk. The phenobarbital helped with her seizures but made her sleepy. Still, he kept at it, putting her feet down on the sidewalk in front of our house as she stood facing him. She wrapped her hands around Papa's index fingers in what he called a death grip. He walked backwards, telling her that she could do it, she could learn to walk. They went up and down the street. He did this for months as Tim, Eileen, and I played in the front yard. Neighbors tracked her progress.

"Keep at it," Mr. Branson called from across the street when he arrived home from work.

"She'll learn," Mrs. Allison said as she picked up the evening paper on the stoop. By then, the leaves on the birch trees had turned deep yellow and were beginning to fall.

With snow on the sidewalks, icicles hanging from the eves, and Christmas approaching, Mary Jean finally let go of Papa's fingers on one hand and then the other. She took her first steps alone. She was almost three years old. People must have been watching from their windows, because the Bransons, the Kents, and the Allisons came out of their houses without even putting on heavy coats. They gathered around and clapped. I ran over and hugged Mary Jean. Now, maybe, she would catch up and be normal.

Santa left our presents under a tree in our basement in 1961. Papa was proud he had finished the basement, which he said added value to our house. During the fall, he'd glued wood paneling to the cement walls and laid green and red tiles in a checkerboard pattern on the floor. Tim got a toy crane big enough to sit on and ride. I got a nurse's kit and the Little Red Spinning Wheel that I coveted. Commercials on TV showed a girl just my age spinning the plastic wheel and pulling out a lovely braid of yarn. Off camera, I guess, she knit the braid into hats, mittens, and scarves. I wound yarn around the plastic parts and spun the wheel, but the strands were just a tangled mess. It was a huge disappointment.

Papa was excited about getting a home movie camera that year. For indoor shots, he used a light bar that made us squint. Footage from Christmas morning shows Eileen, almost two years old, happily talking into a toy telephone, marching a battery-powered elephant along the floor, and spinning a big top. Mary Jean held her arms high in the air to keep her balance and flapped her hands as she lurched across the room. Then she sat down, looking bewildered, and picked up a baby doll for just a moment.

Home movies taken at Fifty-Two that afternoon show similar differences between Eileen and Mary Jean. Among the toys and clothes under the Christmas tree in the front parlor were two matching toy brooms and dustpans. Eileen immediately picked up a broom and began sweeping. Mary Jean sat on the floor chewing the stick of her broom as she rocked back and forth.

A few weeks later, Mary Jean and Eileen had another joint birthday celebration. Papa's home movie shows a cake with five candles, three on one side and two on the other. The cake sat atop a musical stand that rotated and played Happy Birthday. As we sang, Eileen twirled the cake. Mary Jean stuck her fingers in the frosting and, tasting the sweetness, swiped handfuls and then grabbed a candle and stuck it in her mouth. Mom, busy handing out pieces of cake, didn't notice. Eileen ate with a spoon as Mary Jean used her hands to stuff cake in her mouth.

In late January, Mom took Eileen and Mary Jean to our pediatrician for their check-ups. Though my seventh birthday was two months away, I went to get my exam taken care of early. Mom was worried that I was too short for my age and said she'd feel better if we had the doctor check me out.

"Mary Jean is walking!" Mom proudly told Dr. Porter when he came in the room.

The nurse measured my height and made me stand on a scale, then the doctor shined a light in my eyes and looked in my ears and throat. He listened to my chest with a stethoscope.

"Sharon is fine," Dr. Porter said. "You and your husband aren't tall people, so what do you expect?"

Next, he examined Eileen and said that she seemed to be a normal, healthy child.

"Now, let's see this walking, Mary Jean," he said in a cheerful voice. "Mother?"

Mom moved Mary Jean from her lap to the floor. Mary Jean immediately flopped on her bottom.

"Walk, Mary Jean," Mom said, pulling her up by the arms. "Show the doctor that you can walk!"

When Mary Jean didn't move, the doctor picked her up and put her on the exam table.

"Mary Jean, push my hand away," he said.

Mary Jean stared straight ahead. He clapped his hands close to Mary Jean's ear. She jerked her head away from him.

"Her hearing seems normal," he said. "How many words does she have now?

"Fifteen," Mom said, pulling the list from her pocketbook.

"And does she play with the other children?"

"No, she is very quiet and keeps to herself."

"Let's have her try walking again," Dr. Porter said.

This time, Mary Jean stood. She bent her arms up at the elbows, curled her fists, and took a few steps on stiff legs.

Then she opened her hands and spread her fingers wide apart, jerked her hands backwards, and sat.

"Hmmm," he said. "I'm not sure what's wrong with her. It seems that her muscles may be spastic. It's time to have her seen by specialists. I'll set up an appointment at Children's Hospital in Boston. Wait here. I'll have my nurse make a call and then she'll come in and tell you the date."

After Dr. Porter left the room Mom began crying. I took a teddy bear out of a toy box and made it dance to entertain my sisters. Mom was blowing her nose when the nurse came with information written on a yellow notecard. The appointment was four weeks away.

That night Mom told Papa the examination would take two days. Boston was a three-hour drive from our house, so they'd spend a night in a hotel. The rest of us kids would stay with Nana and Gramp.

"I guess it will give us answers," Papa said. "I'll tell my boss tomorrow that I need time off from work. Not exactly how I want to spend my vacation days."

Our time at Fifty-Two while Mom and Papa took Mary Jean to Boston wasn't as much fun as I expected, even though Nana let us have Coke and Freihofer's chocolate chip cookies while she graded spelling tests for the first-graders she taught at Dawes School. Instead of telling us stories or walking down to the convenience store for popsicles, the grown-ups whispered to each other, the wrinkles on their faces pulling the corners of their mouths into frowns.

Aunt El didn't touch the piano once and crocheted row after row, stopping only when she noticed Eileen wandering with a confused look on her face from kitchen to parlor and back again.

"Come here, my little chippie." Aunt El had a special place in heart for Eileen. She pulled Eileen onto her lap and cuddled her. Eileen sighed with contentment.

Gramp, who made his living driving around Berkshire County selling auto parts to service stations, spent a lot of time in the cellar organizing his merchandise. After it got dark on the second day, way past our bedtimes, Mom and Papa came to pick us up. I hugged Mom's legs, but she didn't hug me back.

"Were you well-behaved?" Papa asked. "We brought you presents, but you can only have them if you were good."

Nana nodded that yes, we were good. She was humming, which she did when she was nervous. We sat on the living room floor and pulled gifts out of the Filene's Department Store bag — Matchbox cars for Tim, a baby doll for Eileen that she called "the Boston doll," and a Bobbsey Twins book for me.

"Well?" Gramp asked.

Papa shook his head and said, "Later."

"Those were two of the worst days of my life," Mom said when, pregnant with my first child, I asked about our family's medical history. "We waited for hours as the doctors did tests and watched Mary Jean through a two-way mirror. They told us to go get lunch, so we went to a coffee shop and then to Filene's to distract ourselves."

On the second day, the doctor didn't look at them or say anything for a long time after entering the exam room.

"I couldn't stand it anymore and demanded that he tell us if they'd found a diagnosis," Mom told me. "Finally he said, 'It appears to be severe mental retardation.' Right away I asked if we could keep her at home. He said that she can stay at home as long as things remain the way they are now."

A deep heaviness hung over our house after the trip to Boston. I heard Mrs. Sullivan, a lady in the bridge club, say Mom looked like she had the weight of the world on her shoulders. She whispered the word depression. I didn't know what she meant. The only depression I'd heard about was the one in the 1930s when my parents were kids and my grandfathers were out of work.

I was almost seven and did my best to take care of things around the house. When Mary Jean screamed while Mom made supper, I'd drag the stepstool to the stove and stir whatever was cooking in the skillet. After we ate, I squirted dish soap into the sink and washed the dishes. I didn't mind changing the babies' diapers. The messy ones had a stinky smell, so I held my breath while I rinsed them in the toilet before putting them in the diaper pail to soak with 20 Mule Team Borax. I folded laundry, put away toys, and dusted the furniture. Mom told Nana that I could straighten up the house faster than she could. I was proud to be a good worker.

4

HARDLY HUMAN

During the first half of the 20th century, most Americans believed it was better not to speak of people with developmental disabilities. It was as if they did not exist. But in 1950, the acclaimed author Pearl S. Buck disclosed that she had a thirty-year-old daughter who "had never grown mentally beyond her early childhood." The novelist James Michener was Pearl's neighbor and friend in rural Pennsylvania. "It was whispered that this girl was so retarded that she had been spirited away in some refuge for such children," he wrote in the foreword to the second edition of Pearl's memoir, *The Child Who Never Grew*. The revelation "opened to public discussion a problem that had been previously kept as a shameful secret in the closet of more families than you ever could have anticipated. It was one of the most influential books she wrote."

Pearl and her husband were university professors in China when their first child, Carol, was born in 1920. Pearl was slower to recognize Carol's delayed development than my parents were with Mary Jean. It was not until Carol was four years old that Pearl finally understood that something was very wrong. She begged doctors to answer the same questions my parents asked four decades later: What caused this? Why our family? Is it our fault? What if something happens to me? Who will take care of her after we're gone? Should we find her a place where she can live with others like her? In both the 1920s and the 1960s, there were no clear answers.

Pearl wrote that all the pride in parenthood was gone. She experienced the wish, the same one later voiced by my father, that God would step in and end a child's life: "How often did I cry out in my heart that it would be better if my child had died!" And she experienced depression, which would also envelop my mother: "There was no more joy left in anything," she wrote. "All human relationships became meaningless. Everything became meaningless. I took no more pleasure in the things I enjoyed before; landscapes, flowers, music were empty. Indeed, I could not bear to hear music at all."

When Carol was nine years old, Pearl returned to the United States and toured numerous state-run and private schools. She finally settled on the Training School at Vineland in southern New Jersey, which she judged best for her daughter. Vineland prohibited visits for the first month after placement. Pearl wrote: "Of that month I need not speak. Any parent like me will know the doubts that beset me. . . . These times came in the night, and only the thought of a future with the child grown old and me gone could keep me from hurrying to the nearest railway station."

Pearl, divorced by then, moved from China to Pennsylvania so that she could visit Carol often. Proceeds from her book sales enabled her to give the school endowment funds for the yellow brick cottage where Carol lived.

After Pearl shared her story, first in *Ladies Home Journal* and then as a memoir, she received thousands of letters from parents of children with mental retardation, the term used at the time for what we now call intellectual disabilities. Some desperate parents showed up at her farmhouse door, pleading for guidance. She responded with grace and kindness in an era when professionals often lacked compassion and knowledge.

When Mary Jean was diagnosed in 1962, doctors and clergy still advised parents to put retarded children in an institution and forget them. Experts said the stress of caring for a retarded child would cause grave psychiatric harm to parents and any siblings. For the sake of the family, institutionalization was the logical decision, and it was better not to think or talk about it once the child was placed. A handbook for parents of mentally retarded children is blasé about the impact of an intellectual disability on the individual and dispassionate about the best solution: "The tragedy of mental retardation strikes the parents much harder than it does the child. In fact, the more retarded the child, the less he realizes his condition. More often than not, he is blissfully unaware of the cloud under which he is living or the suffering he has innocently inflicted on his family. . . . In the case of a retarded child for whom little can be done, a child who disrupts the life of the family and makes a slave of the mother, parents would do well to institutionalize him."

Dr. Benjamin Spock's *Common Sense Book of Baby and Child Care* was the bible of baby-boom parents. A dog-eared, coffee-stained copy sat on our family's kitchen counter next to the phone book. Most of the book discussed food, sleep, and potty-training. Advice about "The Handicapped Child" was tucked into a back chapter. Dr. Spock asserted that a seriously retarded child robbed other children in the family of their mother's attention. "It may be better all around if he is cared for in a special home, boarding school, or institution, beginning as soon as his defectiveness is recognized."

He gave chilling instructions to parents of babies with the condition we now call Down syndrome. Despite the fact that the intellectual disabilities of people with Down syndrome are typically not severe, he wrote, "If the family can afford to place the Mongolian baby in a special home, it is usually recommended that this be done right after birth. . . . If he merely exists at a level that is hardly human, it is much better for the other children and the parents to have him cared for elsewhere."

Dr. Spock's characterization of children with Down syndrome as "hardly human" epitomized the appalling attitude that Pearl Buck attempted to change. She wrote in 1950: "Wise men and women are beginning to reason that it is only common sense to accept the mentally retarded person as part of the human family, and to educate him in the things he can do, so that he may be happy in himself and useful to society." Yet her efforts, and those of other advocates, did not come quickly enough to keep my parents from receiving and acting upon advice from their doctor and priest to institutionalize Mary Jean.

A few weeks after the examination in Boston, Mary Jean's seizures increased to three or four a week. She stopped using almost all of the words she'd learned. She spit out most of the food we spooned into her mouth. She'd only eat bits of baked chicken, spaghetti sauce, and mashed potatoes. Nana often stopped by our house with covered dishes of chicken and mashed potatoes and cans of Chef Boyardee sauce. By late winter, a day came when Mary Jean ate nothing at all.

On Mary Jean's second day without food, Mom and Papa brought her to our pediatrician. I went along because I was due for a shot, and a neighbor babysat for Tim and Eileen. The office smelled like the cold alcohol the nurse swabbed on my skin before sticking in the needle. While we waited for the doctor, I sat in a small blue wooden chair in the corner of the room. Mom and Papa stood on either side of the exam table, my father's hands on Mary Jean's shoulders as she sat quietly on a strip of white paper the nurse had smoothed over crackled brown leather padding.

Dr. Porter walked in. Papa explained that Mary Jean had stopped eating. Mom's eyes were red.

"What should we do next?" Papa asked.

"Mary Jean can't survive at home," the doctor said. "She will die if you don't place her in Belchertown."

Suddenly there was another smell in the stuffy room. It seemed to come from Mom. It was like bad breath, or chicken bones left overnight in the garbage can. Mom gripped Papa's arm and shook her head: "No. No, no, no, no, NO!"

But Dr. Porter was firm that Belchertown State School was the only option.

"She can't function in a family with smart children," he said. "She's starving herself to death. In an institution they know how to take care of children like Mary Jean."

My face felt hot. I had trouble catching my breath, like I'd been running really fast. When I got straight-As on my first-grade report card, Papa had told me I was getting too smart for my britches. I talked too much, asked too many questions, butted into adult conversations. Dr. Porter had said Mary Jean couldn't survive in a family with smart children. It was my fault that Mary Jean had to be sent away.

After we got home from the doctor's office, Papa called the rectory of our parish, Sacred Heart Church, and made an appointment to speak to a priest.

"Saturday at 10 a.m.," he said to Mom after he hung up the phone. "Can you get your mother to watch the kids?"

Sacred Heart was the church where we went to mass on Sunday. People called it the pink church because it was painted the color of Pepto-Bismol diarrhea medicine. Every Saturday night Mom plastered my head with green Dippity-Do gel and wound my hair tightly on hard plastic curlers. The curlers dug into my scalp and I had trouble falling asleep. Mom said it was very important for me to look pretty for church, but my thin, straight hair would be limp and only slightly wavy by the time the priest gave the sermon. When I complained that the curlers didn't work, Mom just used more Dippity-Do and rolled the curlers tighter.

When the babies were little, Mom and Papa went to separate masses, and one or the other would take Tim and me. With Mom, we always sat near a door at the end of an aisle. She wanted to be able to leave without anyone seeing her if she started feeling like she would faint. She often became ill in church — perhaps because she couldn't eat or drink anything except water before taking communion at mass — and she hated the idea of people looking at her.

On the Saturday of their appointment with the priest, Nana and Grampa arrived at our house with Dunkin' Donuts. We sat at the kitchen table grabbing our favorites, but Mom said her stomach was queasy. She went to the bathroom and stayed a long time. Finally, she came out wearing cherry-red lipstick. It was smeared a little bit at the corner of her mouth.

Mom and Papa were gone for a long time. When they came home, Papa said that God was testing their faith. Mom's eyes were red from crying. She said Mary Jean would be going to Belchertown very soon.

In the home movies from Easter Sunday that year, Tim sported a red jacket and cap. My sisters and I wore fancy flowered hats. Tim and I waved at the camera, and Eileen scurried away. Mary Jean sucked her thumb, listless as Mom swayed back and forth, cuddling her.

The move to Belchertown was supposed to happen quickly, but we kids got chickenpox, and the institution wouldn't take Mary Jean until her scabs healed. After we recovered from the scratching and headaches and crankiness, the day arrived when Mom and Papa took Mary Jean away.

Standing by the kitchen door, I looked through the screen inches from my nose. If I squinted at all the little wires that kept flies out, I could see hundreds of tiny gray squares. I tried to count them, but my eyes blurred with tears. Papa lifted Mary Jean's skeletal body into the back seat of the station wagon that we called the new car, even though he'd bought it used through a classified ad in *The Berkshire Eagle*. Mom, wearing a navy-and-white polka dot dress with a navy belt, got in the front passenger seat. Papa slid in behind the wheel. He looked over his shoulder and backed out the driveway. Mom stared straight ahead. No one waved goodbye.

Nana, babysitting for the day, turned to follow Eileen, who ran toward the living room dragging a blanket. Tim and I didn't touch, didn't talk. After the car disappeared down the street, he went into the backyard.

I stood alone at the door for a long time, feeling lonely and ashamed. If I hadn't been so smart, maybe Mary Jean could have stayed at home.

5

PRAYING THAT GOD WILL TAKE HER

At Belchertown, just like the school where Pearl Buck's daughter was institutionalized, family visits were prohibited for the first month after a resident placement, allegedly to ease the adjustment. Although we had beautiful spring weather, it was a hard, gloomy month. It seemed like the color had gone out of our lives. I picked violets that bloomed against the cellar wall, wrapped the stems in damp paper towels covered with aluminum foil, and gave them to Mom. The bouquets didn't keep her from crying a lot.

Papa was almost always angry. "You're too rambunctious," he'd snarl when Tim and Eileen played on the living room floor. "Quiet down."

Typically, I sat silently on the couch reading. I could never figure out what to do or say to make my parents happy.

My greatest joy was the time that I spent with Gramp after school was over. Because the Sacred Heart parish school was still under construction, I took a city bus from Birch Grove Drive to downtown Pittsfield to attend first grade at Notre Dame School. It was a little scary, and the bus smelled bad from diesel exhaust, but I wasn't alone. Other kids from our neighborhood went to Notre Dame, too. The nuns made us learn prayers in French: *Au nom du Pére et du Fils et du Saint-Esprit. Amen. In the name of the Father, and of the Son, and of the Holy Spirit. Amen.* The rest of our lessons were in English.

At three o'clock, I'd load my canvas bag with the books I'd need for homework and head down Melville Street toward the bus stop on the far side of North Street. Once in a while, Gramp would be waiting on the sidewalk halfway down the block.

"Sherry," he'd call to me. "That bookbag is bigger than you are!"

He'd sling the bag over his shoulder and envelop my small hand with his.

"How about a Coke?" he'd ask.

We'd walk into the Sugar Bowl on the corner. He had to help me climb onto a tall stool at the counter. Gramp and I would talk about my day and what I was doing in class. I felt proud about learning to read a few weeks into the school year.

The first time we went to the Sugar Bowl together after Mary Jean went to Belchertown, I told him how much I missed her. Not the screaming or the seizures, but I missed seeing her in the crib when I went into the babies' room. I missed trying to charm her into eating a bite of mashed potatoes. I wondered what she was doing at Belchertown. Was she lonely? Scared? Did she have a doll or a ball? Maybe we could bring her a toy when we visited.

"You have a big heart, Sherry," Gramp said. "You're a tiny girl with a big heart and a big mind."

I shook my head no, frustrated that I couldn't figure out a way for Mary Jean to stay at home. Gramp was silent. I looked at him and his blue eyes were wet with tears.

"Ah, Sherry," he finally said. "It's not your fault."

He was trying to make me feel better but I knew, beyond any doubt, it was my fault that Mary Jean had to be sent away.

After four long weeks, we could finally visit Belchertown. We went to Sunday mass all together to save time and left straight from church. The drive took about an hour and a half on winding roads through the hill towns of eastern Berkshire County and down into the Connecticut River valley. We passed a grassy town common and at last came to a brick sign: Belchertown State School.

"Isn't this pretty?" Mom said as we parked under a maple tree. "It looks almost like a college campus."

Bored from the long car ride, Tim and I quickly picked up wing-like maple tree seeds and pretended they were helicopters, holding them high over our heads and throwing them with shouts of "whirlybird, whirlybird." Eileen sat on the grass at the edge of the parking lot, making a tiny pile of the dried-out seeds.

"Get up, Eileen," Papa said sternly. "Keep your clothes clean. Settle down, you two." Tim put a whirlybird in his pocket as I pulled Eileen up from the ground and brushed dirt from her bottom. We quietly followed Mom and Papa toward huge stone steps leading up to the brick administration building. I looked up at a giant clock tower on the roof — it was 11:30.

Papa gave his name to a secretary at the front desk, who made a phone call.

"Wait there," she said, pointing to a corner of the lobby. We stood for about twenty minutes. Bored, I sounded out the sign above a door — Lawrence Bowser, M.D., Superintendent. A bald man with glasses walked through the door and spoke sharply to the secretary. Bow-ser, I thought, unkindly. He doesn't say bow-wow like a dog, but he looks like a bulldog.

Finally, an attendant arrived with Mary Jean, who smiled as Papa reached out and hugged her to his chest. Mom gave Mary Jean a kiss as the woman brusquely reported that Mary Jean was saying a few words and eating again.

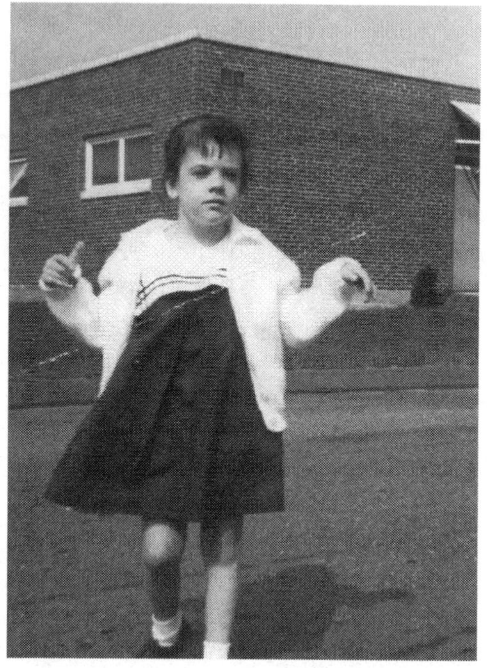

Mary Jean —
Belchertown State School, about 1962

"Kiss your sister," Papa said, and we all pecked her cheek before returning to the car. Papa put Mary Jean in the middle of the back seat. Tim, Eileen and I fought for the window seats.

"Settle down," Papa said. "Let Eileen stand next the window. Just move your feet, Sharon." That was before the days of seat belts and car seats.

We went to The Dairy Bar for lunch. The waitress, accustomed to families coming in with their retarded children, was nice. We didn't often eat out, so going to The Dairy Bar was a special treat. I got a cheeseburger and black cherry ice cream, which is like vanilla, but with big chunks of icy fruit. After lunch, we played on the town common. Mom laughed and shook her head close to Mary Jean's face, trying to coax a smile. Papa sat on the grass and wrestled gently with Mary Jean. A couple times she pushed him over and giggled.

"It's getting late," Papa said after a while, and we piled in the car to take Mary Jean back.

"I think we made the right decision to place her here," Mom said as we drove away from the school. But her eyes were wet.

A week later, it was the same routine. The drive from the Berkshires into the Connecticut River valley was familiar this time. In the decades before the Revolutionary War, when soldiers and missionaries from the Boston area traveled west to fight or convert the Mohicans, this region of the state became known as the Berkshire Barrier. Although the mountains are not particularly high, rivers cut deep valleys that made travel with a horse and wagon hard. The roads curve and dip to avoid rock outcroppings and ancient trees too big for the early settlers to clear.

Because we'd been there before, we were allowed to pick up Mary Jean at the nursery building where she lived. A woman unlocked the door and led us into a hallway. It smelled like the dirty bathrooms we had to use in gas stations when we traveled to Ohio.

"Wait here," she said.

"Can we see Mary Jean's room?" I asked.

"Visitors are only allowed in the lobby. An attendant will bring Mary Jean from the ward."

"Is that the ward?" I asked, pointing through a half-opened door.

"Be quiet," Papa hissed.

"That's the day room," the woman said.

Before she slammed the door shut, I saw young girls sitting in rows of chairs. One put her hands in her underpants and wiped poop on her shirt. I'd changed babies' diapers, but I'd never seen people touch their own poop. I felt scared and embarrassed. I concentrated on learning more about Mary Jean's building.

"What's a ward?" I asked.

Mom and Papa ignored my question. Tim rolled a Matchbox car back and forth on the black-and-white tile floor, an engine noise coming deep from his throat. Eileen cuddled her stuffed elephant tightly against her chest. I stood in silence, afraid to upset Mom and Papa. When the huge door opened again, the sounds of children's yells filled the waiting room. Glancing at Tim and Eileen without moving my head, I could tell all three of us were trying in vain to block memories of Mary Jean's screams when she lived at home. A second woman gripped Mary Jean's thin arm and shoved her toward Mom.

Mary Jean had nasty purple bumps on her forehead.

"Did she fall?" Mom gasped.

"Mary Jean bangs her head against the wall," the attendant said.

"And the scabs on her arms?" Papa asked.

"She bites them, and they bleed. Sometimes this happens during the adjustment period."

Mary Jean walked toward Mom with slow, wobbly steps. She winced each time she put weight on a foot. When Mom squatted and reached out with welcoming arms, Mary Jean kicked her shin hard. Mom gasped and stood up. Mary Jean came at her again, kicking and shrieking.

"Mary Jean. Mary Jean. I love you, Mary Jean," Mom sobbed, paralyzed by her belief that nothing could be done when Mary Jean acted out. The doctors who recommended forgetting that retarded children had ever been born did not offer parents the intervention strategies available today.

Mary Jean twisted away from Mom and stumbled toward me. She hit my face, hard. It hurt, but I was determined not to cry. I had to be strong and help Mom.

"Mary Jean," I said. "I love you, too."

Tim backed away. Eileen looked confused.

"Foot?" Eileen said. "Mary Jean's foot hurts!"

Mary Jean swung her arm and gave Eileen a brutal punch to the chest. When Tim tried to step between them, Mary Jean landed a fierce kick on Tim's leg.

"She's just getting used to things," Papa said firmly. "Give her time."

Scooping up Mary Jean in his arms, Papa walked toward the exit.

"Let's get going. In the car, everyone," he barked. "Jean, it's not the time to fall apart."

Mom bit her lip. With a stiff arm, she gestured for us to follow Papa. I felt hot, like I had a fever. I didn't know what to do. I wanted to take care of Mom, to make her feel better, to keep her from making Papa mad with her soft, sniffling cries. I was angry that I hadn't done better at not acting smart so that Mary Jean could have stayed at home.

When we got to the car, Tim, Eileen, and I wiggled in and didn't say a word about who sat where. Before Papa started the engine, Mary Jean reached forward and pulled hard on Mom's hair.

"Ow!" Mom yelped. "Paul, do something!" Mom cried in big, loud gulps.

"Let's try putting her in the front seat," Papa said in a tight voice.

We all got out of the car. Papa lifted Mary Jean into the front seat and Mom squeezed in the back. None of us spoke. Once again, Papa drove to The Dairy Bar.

"Be careful in the parking lot," Papa said as we left the car. Mom walked quickly ahead of us. Papa carried Mary Jean. Tim and Eileen followed close behind me. Not a word was needed to keep us in line.

We went inside and the waitress told us to take whatever booth we wanted. Eileen sat on one side with Papa and Mary Jean, and Mom sat with Tim and me on the other side. I think Mom was afraid to let Mary Jean sit close enough to pull her hair again.

"Order the same thing as you did last week," Papa said. "We don't want to waste time."

The waitress brought our Cokes. Before I'd even unwrapped my straw, Mary Jean tipped over her glass. It didn't break, but Coke spread out over the table and dripped onto the vinyl bench. She let out a long, loud shriek when Papa put napkins against her chest. Mom and I mopped up the mess with more napkins.

After the burgers arrived, Papa told us to hurry and finish our food.

"I haven't even had one bite," I protested. "How can I hurry up?"

"Don't mouth off," he snapped.

"Sharon…" Mom said in a low voice, barely moving her lips.

"It's just that it's not…" I was going to say "fair," but I could see a blood vessel popping up on Papa's forehead, and I knew I had to shut up.

Papa wolfed down his burger in a few bites. Eileen scooted as far away from Papa and Mary Jean as possible. I ate as quickly as I could. Every time I swallowed, it felt like the food got stuck in my chest. Mary Jean continued her loud yelping noises.

"Can we get ice cream?" Tim asked.

"Absolutely not," Papa said.

"What about cones to take in the car?" Tim said.

"I said no!" Every time he spoke, Papa's voice got louder. Mom's face was white. Mary Jean yanked Eileen's hair. Eileen hid her face in the corner of the booth, quickly quieting her sobs. Papa carried Mary Jean to the parking lot while Mom paid the bill.

"Are we going to play on the town common again?" I asked.

"No, Mary Jean is having a bad day, so we'll bring her back now," Papa said.

When we arrived at Mary Jean's building, Papa took her inside while we waited in the car. There was hardly any talking during the long drive home to Pittsfield.

"I pray that God will just take her," Papa said in a deep, angry voice, echoing Pearl Buck's wish for her daughter. Mom, who'd been crying quietly, sobbed harder.

God take her? Did Papa want her to die?

"I'm gonna be sick," I said.

Papa pulled the car over by the side of the road. I jumped out and threw up in a pile of dead leaves. Mom gave me a crumbled-up tissue from her pocketbook to wipe my mouth and chin. No one said anything.

When we got home, our next-door neighbors were in their front yard.

"How was Mary Jean?" Mrs. Kent asked. "Did you find her well?"

"Everything is just fine," Papa said, smiling. "Mary Jean is doing very well. We made the right decision to place her in Belchertown."

I went in the house and threw up again.

Every week, we drove to Belchertown after mass on Sunday. Every week, Mary Jean was blood-stained and bruised. And every week, Papa stopped the car on the way home for one or more of us kids to throw up. It was a terrible summer.

That fall, I started second grade at Sacred Heart School, my third school in as many years. The building was new and smelled of paint and floor wax. Most of the nuns were old, though. When the teachers and students gathered for the first-day-of-school rosary in the multi-purpose room, Sister Superior announced that we were heathens, and she would snap us into shape.

I tried really hard to be good and obey all the rules, except for one. Each class was assigned a section of the black-topped parking lot for recess. We weren't supposed to leave our sections, but the first thing I did was check on Tim in the corner where the first-graders played. The nuns called me a mother hen. At home, Tim and Eileen complained I was bossy. Papa said I was a worrywart. No one understood. I just wanted to keep the younger kids safe. I was afraid that something would happen that would make them retarded, too.

Papa said it was important to visit often to keep Mary Jean a part of our family, even though she didn't understand how much time passed between visits. Eventually, our weekly visits to Belchertown became every other week. Waiting for Mary Jean in the nursery building lobby, we heard children screaming and banging in the dayroom. The smells of filthy diapers and stale food became routine.

Every visit seemed the same. Mary Jean's blank stare, her mouth hung open. Bruises blotching her forehead and face. Cuts and scabs covering her arms. Her hard kicks against Mom's shin and a yank to her hair. Mom's lips trembling and her eyes filling with tears.

Mary Jean looked like the frail toddler she was, yet she lashed out with incredible strength. She was unable to talk normally. She'd parrot our names when Papa instructed "Say Sharon" or "Say Mom." Sometimes she'd repeat, "love you." If she was calm, she'd accept an "Eskimo kiss," with one of us rubbing our nose against hers.

We'd take her to The Dairy Bar or to the sloping fields overlooking Quabbin Reservoir, just east of Belchertown, for a picnic. We'd eat baloney sandwiches and drink cans of root beer or cola. I hated baloney — especially when it was warm from being in the car — and I didn't like the discount sodas Papa bought as a special treat, either. When I said Coca Cola and Hire's root beer tasted better, he said the name brands that Nana bought cost too much, and we should be grateful to have soda at all.

After we ate, Tim and Eileen played tag or looked for four-leaf clovers. Mary Jean had trouble walking on the grass, so she sat on Papa's lap. Once in a while she was calm enough to let Mom hold her. I read or looked at the water. I found the reservoir kind of creepy. Papa told us that during the Great Depression, the state made people abandon their houses so that the land could be flooded for the reservoir. Whole towns disappeared. They even dug up dead people from the cemeteries and moved them to higher ground. I stared at the water, wondering if they'd missed any graves. Maybe a skeleton would wash up on the shore.

Papa with Mary Jean —
Town Common, Belchertown, about 1964

Every trip to Belchertown was a reminder of how much I missed my sister. Even though her seizures were scary and her screaming disruptive, Belchertown was so horrible that I wanted her to live with us. I was certain that she hit and kicked because she was angry at being sent away, but Papa said she was too retarded to know the difference between home and the institution. Yet he pounded it into our heads that we were a family, and we should think about Mary Jean every day and include her in our prayers every night. When people asked how many kids were in our family, we were schooled to include Mary Jean — but then it was embarrassing to explain why our sister didn't live at home.

6

MISS SMARTY PANTS

During the 18th and 19th centuries, in a nation founded on possibilities and hope, people with intellectual and developmental disabilities were called idiots, imbeciles, and simpletons. We locked them in cellars, closets, and cages.

When I was a teenager, Mom told me about a family who lived on her street when she was growing up.

"The McKennas had a child who never developed physically or mentally beyond babyhood. Most people didn't know of the child's existence, but I remember Mrs. McKenna walking the baby after dark in the back yard," she said. "It was a shameful thing to have a defective child. People always blamed the mother."

Mom took a deep breath and wiped tears from the corners of her eyes.

During the middle of the 19th century, a few educational reformers tried to change things. Dorothea Dix, a Boston school teacher, and Dr. Samuel Gridley Howe, a Massachusetts state legislator and the founder of the Perkins Institute for the Blind, wrote passionate articles and delivered fiery lectures, trying to convince their fellow citizens that "idiots" could be trained to "industry, order, and self-respect." In 1848, the state awarded Howe $2,500 for a three-year experimental school to teach "ten idiotic children."

The scientific principles that Dix and Howe developed were widely rejected by fellow citizens and legislators. By the end of the 19th century, the state converted what had once been small, progressive schools in Massachusetts into large asylums. Howe decried "permanent life asylums as unnatural, undesirable, and leading to abuse and the severing of the inmates' ties to kin, friends, and neighborhood."

Progressive efforts largely came to a halt after the eugenics movement grew in popularity during the early 20th century. Sir Francis Galton, a half-cousin of Charles Darwin, coined the word eugenics from the Greek *eugenes*, which means well born. Galton believed that people could promote the highest quality of human being by eliminating the unfit through better breeding. Proponents argued that feeble-mindedness was highly hereditary and sterilizing inferior people would improve the genetic quality of the human population. They urged state legislators to expand the number of state-funded institutions, arguing that segregation was the best way to prevent breeding.

In 1904, American doctors seized on an intelligence tool developed by French psychologist Alfred Binet that measured a child's degree of advancement or retardation against a norm. Binet's intent was to identify children in need of special instruction. Much to his horror, U.S. doctors used his work to support their claim that intelligence is fixed and deficiencies immutable. Historian R.C. Scheerenberger wrote that in 1909, Binet "spoke out strongly against the 'brutal pessimism' of persons who believed that intelligence was a fixed quantity that could not be increased." However, Binet was unsuccessful in shifting the thinking of American physicians toward a more positive use of his assessment.

In 1915, the Massachusetts State Board of Insanity responded to public desire to isolate retarded people and appropriated $50,000 to buy land for a new asylum in a rural location. The Board of Trade in Belchertown, a village about eighty miles west of Boston, expended great effort to secure the institution. The next year, a newspaper article announcing that Belchertown was awarded the new school noted, "There is a growing recognition of the hereditary nature of much mental defect and the necessity of segregating cases likely to transmit the defect." Surprisingly, the townspeople didn't object to living in proximity to the institution. In fact, the school soon became Belchertown's largest employer.

The state purchased more than 800 acres of farmland. Construction began in 1918. The campus became a town within a town as the state built red brick dormitories, classrooms, a hospital, a dental clinic, and a power plant. The school had its own water, sewage, and telephone systems, and a fire department. The campus featured winding lanes and views of lush fields. Buildings were set far apart from one another. Belchertown State School for the Feeble-Minded opened in 1922.

The Massachusetts Department of Mental Diseases, the new name of the State Board of Insanity, operated the school. Children, women, and men with a wide range of developmental and physical disabilities lived in buildings divided into wards. As was the case when Mary Jean lived there, a typical bedroom area contained forty beds, with no privacy partitions or space for personal belongings. A side room housed the residents' clothing.

Although it was called a school, Belchertown wasn't really that. Dr. Walter Fernald, superintendent of Belchertown's sister school, the Massachusetts School for the Feeble-Minded in Waltham, had delivered a highly influential address in 1912. He made the case that "the feeble-minded are a parasitic, predatory class" that must be institutionalized to prevent reproduction. Fernald argued that the public must be informed about "the extent, causation, and significance" of feeble-mindedness; his goal was to secure funding for institutions, not to provide education for the feeble-minded themselves.

Doctors at Belchertown classified residents by mental age using Binet's assessment. "Idiots" had mental ages between ages birth and three; they were considered untrainable and confined in locked wards. "Imbeciles" had mental ages between four and seven and could be trained. "Morons" had mental ages between seven and twelve years. Although "morons" were supposed to be educated, inadequate funding and frequent budget cuts often meant that no teachers were available at Belchertown.

Residents did much of the work — without pay — in the kitchens, laundry, butchery, cannery, bakery, carpentry shop, print shop, shoe repair shop, sawmill, and industrial and maintenance buildings. Female residents ages sixteen and older took care of younger children and cleaned the buildings, including the administrators' homes. Adult male residents cultivated 200 acres of land and managed a herd of registered cattle and large poultry flocks. On weekends the attendants led residents to the massive auditorium for movies and live shows put on by local theater troupes.

For most of its history, Belchertown State School was understaffed and overcrowded, with one worker responsible for fifty or more residents. Pay was low compared to other jobs that required a similar level of training. Rules tightly controlled day-to-day life. Residents suffered severe punishments — withholding food and water, or weeks of solitary confinement — for deviation from the regulations.

The year that Mary Jean entered Belchertown, a panel appointed by President John F. Kennedy released its "National

Plan to Combat Mental Retardation." The president had a personal connection to the subject; his younger sister Rosemary was mentally retarded. The panel made more than 100 recommendations for a comprehensive federal approach to improve care and services, calling on Kennedy to "think and plan boldly."

In February 1963, Kennedy's "Special Message to the Congress on Mental Illness and Mental Retardation" proposed a move from custodial institutions to community-centered agencies. He called for the construction of research centers that would include diagnostic, clinical, and treatment services; new programs for maternity and prenatal care; and an expansion of special education, training, and rehabilitation.

In October of that same year, Kennedy signed two bills that set the stage for states to partner with the federal government to improve services. The Maternal and Child Health and Mental Retardation Planning Amendments of 1963 authorized federal grants to assist states in developing comprehensive plans to mitigate the negative impacts of mental retardation. The Mental Retardation Facilities and Community Mental Health Centers Construction Act of 1963 established a formula grant program that provided states with federal dollars to build community-based facilities. This was the first time the federal government established a partnership with states to administer federal funds related to mental retardation.

At a ceremony to celebrate the signing of these landmark bills, Kennedy spoke about the imperative to expand government support: "The mentally ill and the mentally retarded need no longer be alien to our affections or beyond the help of our communities."

If my parents were aware of any of these developments, I don't remember them talking about it. They were single-minded about a different kind of progress. After Mary Jean went to

Belchertown, my parents' focus was on fashioning a nice home. Every time they saved up a bit of money, they did something to improve our house on Birch Grove Drive. Papa built a corner cabinet in the dining room to display their ivory wheat-patterned ironstone dinnerware. The maroon color he used for the first coat was too dark for their taste, so he blended in pale gray paint until he got the perfect cranberry shade.

"The dishes look lovely against the maroon," he said to Mom.

"Very upscale," Mom replied with a satisfied smile.

Papa cut down a tree to make room for a garage with a breezeway to the kitchen door. After refusing offers of help from men in the neighborhood — "Do they think I'm not capable?!" — he pulled a muscle in his back while yanking out tree roots from the ground. He staggered into the kitchen, his hands still covered with dirt, and passed out before he made it to the couch.

"Paul!" Mom screamed. "Sharon, run next door and get Mrs. Kent! I'll call for an ambulance!"

Mrs. Kent was a nurse. She rushed to our house wearing an apron over her plaid pants, wiping her wet hands on a towel. She knelt next to Papa and grabbed his wrist.

"His pulse is fast and thready," she said.

Mom sobbed, tears running down her face: "Please, God, don't let him die."

Mr. Kent and another neighbor decided to take Papa to the hospital in the back of the Kent's station wagon, figuring it would be faster than an ambulance. I worried Papa would be unhappy with this plan, remembering his comments that the Kents' Country Squire station wagon was expensive and the wood side-paneling pretentious. Papa was barely conscious when the men put him in the back. Mrs. Kent climbed in back, too, saying that she would keep checking Papa's pulse. Mom called my grandparents as soon as they drove away.

"Mum, I need you and Dad to come right away," she said, panicked. "It's Paul. I need you to watch the children."

She dropped the phone when a police officer banged on the front door.

"You called for an ambulance?" he asked. Two men carrying a stretcher stood on the front lawn.

"Yes, for my husband, but our neighbors already left with him. They're heading for the hospital."

"That was really stupid, ma'am," the officer said. "These men have special training. And you just wasted the taxpayers' money calling us out."

Mom started crying again.

"I'm so sorry. I'm so, so sorry. I was just so scared."

Mrs. Kent was a nurse, but would Papa die because he was going to the hospital in a station wagon instead of an ambulance? The officers left, shaking their heads, just as Nana and Gramp pulled up in their blue Chrysler. Gramp drove Mom to the hospital. A few hours later they returned with Papa. He wasn't dead.

"Just a strained muscle," Papa said as he settled onto the couch. Mom tucked a cushion behind his head. "I have an unusual pain threshold, the doctor said. Makes me faint when I'm in pain."

He had to stay home from work for a few days to let his back heal. Tim played fainting to make us laugh. He'd flop on the living room floor and yell, "Oh, my back!"

Papa warned, "Don't make me get up off this couch to get the board of education," which is what he called the wooden paddle he used to spank us. "Settle down."

Chastened, Tim ducked into Eileen's room. Spanking was one thing, but Tim, Eileen, and I often worried that if we didn't behave, we might be sent to Belchertown, too.

The garage was finished by the time we brought Mary Jean home for a Christmas visit that year. Santa brought a small wooden table with two chairs. On the red chair cushions sat three white piggy banks with our names — Tim, Eileen, and Sharon — glued to the sides. The banks were exactly the size and shape as the gallon-sized plastic bottles of bleach that Mom used to do the laundry. Mary Jean, who rocked in a chair as the rest of us opened our presents, didn't get a bank. It gave me a queasy feeling. It seemed like Mary Jean was not a part of our family anymore, even though Papa said we should always keep her in our hearts.

Papa's home movie from that Christmas shows Tim grinning as he hugged what would become his favorite stuffed animal, Sammy the Seal. Mom read the book *Sammy the Seal* almost as often as Eileen's favorite, *The Little Engine That Could*. Eileen loved to scoot up and down our small hallway chanting, "I think I can, I think I can." Mary Jean sat on the floor, holding a clear plastic ball with a toy inside, and didn't protest when Eileen took it away. Instead of picking up another toy, Mary Jean quietly sucked her thumb.

The day after Christmas, we drove Mary Jean back to Belchertown.

Papa put a lot of work into making our house on Birch Grove Drive the way he and Mom wanted it, but he also said it would be a good idea to "take advantage of our equity" to find a bigger house. I didn't know what equity meant, and he ignored me when I asked. On Saturday mornings, he and Mom often sat at the kitchen table drinking an extra cup of coffee and talking about the "house for sale" listings in *The Berkshire Eagle*. I'd hear them say "out of our price range" or "that's been on the market a while," but one day Mom said, "Here's a new one."

Papa took the paper from her. "Look at the size of the lot! Wouldn't hurt to take a look."

He arranged to see the house that afternoon.

Tim, Eileen, and I fought for a window seat. I'm not sure why it really mattered to me, since I brought along a book. I glanced up once and was aware that we were on Peck's Road, the back way to my grandparents' summer cottage. When Papa turned into the driveway, I dropped my book. This was a mansion!

The white house was built atop a small hill and had yellow-and-white striped awnings that shaded an enclosed front porch. The driveway ended in a cul-de-sac, with room to turn a car around. A two-story, two-car garage faced us. To the left was another garage and a shed. Flower gardens ringed the yard.

Mom rang the bell and the owners, Mr. and Mrs. Green, welcomed us in. They told us the house was originally built for the superintendent of the defunct woolen mill down the street. We were the first potential buyers to see the house.

"Very upscale," Mom whispered to Papa as she took in the elaborate wallpaper and Asian furniture. The rooms were big: the kitchen with a pantry area, the dining room with a bay window and walk-in butler's closet, and a living room and a den at the front of the house. The staircase had a landing. Upstairs were three big bedrooms, a bathroom, and a room the Greens called a gentleman's den. The basement had a wine cellar with built-in racks, a cedar-lined walk-in closet, a coal cellar, and lots of room for laundry and storage. Outside again, we opened a wooden gate next to the bigger of the two garages — the owners said it was originally a barn — and realized the property included the back side of the hill, all the way down to a tiny stream. The barn had a hayloft with windows at both ends.

"Cool," Tim said, looking down the hill. We couldn't make our way to the bottom because dead weeds stretched higher than our heads. "We could make tunnels here."

I headed back toward the car, sure Papa would tell us it was time to go. Instead, we went back into the kitchen. Papa talked quietly with the owners.

"Would you take $1.00 in earnest money?" he asked.

Mom opened her pocketbook and put a dollar bill on the table.

"If I could use your phone, I'll call my brother to write up the papers," she said. "He is our attorney."

After Uncle John arrived, the grownups wrote down numbers and dates and signed documents.

"We'll have the rest of the earnest money to you when the bank opens on Monday," Papa said.

He and Mr. Green shook hands. On our way home, we stopped at Nichol's liquor store and loaded empty boxes into the trunk of the car for packing.

We moved into the big house on the hill in the summer of 1963. Mom and Papa paid extra to buy a few pieces of furniture from the Greens. My favorite was the Chinese-red hall table with a matching mirror. By the end of moving day, Mom and Papa had arranged the furniture and frenetically unpacked all the boxes.

"In just one day!" Mom told her parents when they stopped by with donuts the next morning. "We got all this done in just one day!"

I'd never seen her happier. But Nana was not happy.

"Peck's Road is terribly busy," she said. "And this is a very seedy neighborhood. The house is pleasant, but you really should be in a better part of town. Did you think about the parkways? They are so much nicer."

The parkways were an expensive part of town in Sacred Heart parish.

"It's beautiful and has a wonderful yard," Papa said, glaring at Nana. "We'll be able to plant a huge garden in the back."

I later realized a big part of his decision to buy the Peck's Road house was the barn and garden, which provided an outlet for his urge to farm. Unlike his GE job, where his college courses hadn't prepared him for his responsibilities, he felt confident and in charge when he fiddled with the yard equipment and made things grow.

Across the street from our big superintendent's house on the hill were row houses where workers used to live before the mill went out of business. The people who lived in the row houses were poor, just as Nana said. But I loved the new house and didn't care if it was on the wrong side of town. We used the shed as a playroom, and I claimed the hayloft as my reading spot. We rode our bikes in circles at the top of the driveway and down the lawn of the side yard. Papa hung a tire swing from a willow tree, and we soared high over the steep backyard. He hired a man with a bulldozer to scrape the weeds and pile them at the bottom of the hill, creating an enormous compost pile. Papa shoveled dirt from the side of the pile whenever he needed to enrich the garden soil.

Even though Papa loved the new place, the other kids and I still had to be wary of his temper. One day, after reading a story in *The Berkshire Eagle*, he said that a telephone hotline directly between Washington and Moscow would never work.

"A cable that long can't sustain a message," he said with disgust.

"Yes, it can," I replied, full of eight-year-old confidence. "The radio said the U.S. sent a message to Russia, and it worked. It was a silly message — the quick brown fox jumped over the lazy dog's back. It's called a pangram because it used all the letters of the alphabet."

"Don't you dare contradict me," he said, raising his voice.

"But . . ."

He hit my face with a half-closed fist.

"Nobody likes a Miss Smarty Pants. If you keep up your fancy talk, no one will like you, and you'll never get a boyfriend."

His words stung more than my cheek. Even though I was too young for a boyfriend, I didn't have friends in our new neighborhood. Moving to Peck's Road meant changing schools again, but I'd never had close friends. While other kids ran happily on the playground and went to each other's houses on weekends, I was usually too preoccupied about Mary Jean being sent away and Mom's crying to play stupid games. I was afraid that if other kids came to our house, Papa would yell about too much noise and embarrass me. I promised myself that when the school year started, I'd try to not act smart and to smile and play. Maybe people would like me.

I began third grade at St. Charles School in September 1963. Tim and I walked together the nearly mile-and-a-half down Peck's Road, across Wahconah Street and the west branch of the Housatonic River, and up the steep Pontoosuc Avenue hill to the brick school building.

The classrooms smelled like moldy vegetables, the nuns were mean, and I was bored. I got in trouble for looking ahead in the textbook. Getting caught meant a knuckle smack with a wooden ruler and ten Hail Marys on my knees before I could go outside for recess. I joined the funeral choir, even though I've never been able to sing on key, so that I could get out of class every time someone in the parish died. A lot of old people lived in the neighborhood, and I'd soon memorized the Latin hymns of the funeral mass.

On November 22 that year, Sister Superior came into our classroom and ordered everyone to walk single file across the street to the church. After the entire school had assembled, the pastor told us to kneel and pray for our country. President John Fitzgerald Kennedy had been shot and killed in Texas. Gasps turned quickly to tears.

After we all said the rosary together, the pastor said we could go home for the rest of the afternoon. I wasn't sure what might happen after a president was killed. During the Cuban Missile Crisis a year earlier, we did attack drills, hiding under our desks to avoid exposure to radiation. Kids said that Pittsfield's GE Ordinance Plant would make our city the very first target in a nuclear war. Would the Soviet Union attack us now that we didn't have a president? I wished I could take the school bus instead of slogging through the long walk home, but our house was a hundred yards short of the required distance for receiving free bus tickets. Tim was home sick that day, so I had to walk alone. When I finally got home, Mom was in front of the TV, crying. Papa walked in the door a few minutes later, home from work much earlier than usual.

"He was a good man," Papa said.

"He was a very good man," Mom agreed.

After watching the news for a while, Tim went to his room. When he was upset, he preferred to be alone and focus on one of his many interests, which ranged over the years from countless pet turtles, lizards, and fish to CB radios and the birds in Berkshire County. Eileen, almost four years old, was hard-wired to find ways to break the tension.

"Dance! Dance to the piano!" she said, skipping around the room.

"Eileen, stop being a ham," Papa chided her. "This is serious."

Mom and Papa ridiculed her when she acted like a kid and criticized me when I acted like a Miss Smarty Pants. They frequently told Eileen she should be grateful that she had a normal brain and wasn't retarded like Mary Jean. They told me to stop talking so much. Not one of Papa's three daughters met the expectation he had spelled out in a letter to Mom when he was in college: "Of course I want a son first, but if our first turns out to be a daughter, it will be OK because she'll be exactly like you."

Lyndon Johnson was sworn in as president, and we didn't have a nuclear war. We continued to go to Belchertown to see Mary Jean throughout the winter. In the spring, Papa plowed space for a garden at the bottom of the back hill. He took Tim, Eileen, and me with him to Agway, a garden and farming supply store, to buy vegetable seeds and a big burlap bag of seed potatoes. I hated the smell inside the dusty store.

"It really stinks in here," I said.

"That's just manure," Papa said. "Nature's fertilizer. It's a good, clean smell."

I thought he was crazy.

"Don't worry, we don't have to buy manure," he said. "The compost pile will give us all the muck we need."

As a kid, I didn't understand why Eileen liked working in the garden. I later realized that asking questions about farming was her only way to cajole Papa into a good mood. Working alongside him was a safe place to get the attention she craved. I preferred reading, but we were all expected to do our share in the garden.

Pumpkins and gourds were the easiest crops to plant. We just threw handfuls of seeds on top of the compost pile and they grew on their own. For the rest of the garden, Papa taught us to use a string and sticks to make straight lines in the dirt. He made furrows and showed us how to drop in sweet corn and green bean seeds and chunks of potato.

"Every seed potato must have an eye, or nothing will grow," he said with enthusiasm, showing us a small black spot on a wrinkled piece of potato. "The sprout will grow from the eye and make a new plant. If we have a good year, we'll get fifty pounds of potatoes from every row. That will be enough to eat all year and have seed potatoes for next year."

Papa insisted we eat potatoes for dinner every night of the week, except when we had spaghetti. I didn't taste rice until I went to college. Once a week Mom browned hamburger in a skillet, stirred in a can of Campbell's pork and beans, and spooned the mixture over boiled potatoes. Catholics didn't eat meat on Fridays, so Mom heated canned tuna with peas and cream of mushroom soup and ladled it over boiled potatoes. Baked potatoes were served with the occasional London broil or sirloin steak on the grill. Mashed potatoes were for special occasions like Thanksgiving, when Mom splashed boiled potatoes with hot milk and melted butter and whipped them with an electric mixer. Potato salad during the summer was my favorite, made with Hellman's mayonnaise and green olives and chopped hard-boiled eggs. For special picnics, we'd put slices of the egg on top and sprinkle the whole bowl with paprika.

I hated digging potatoes. They weren't ready for harvest until October, when the evenings were cold. At that time of year, Papa went to work an hour earlier than usual, and Mom had supper on the table as soon as he walked through the door at 4:20. We ate quickly and left Mom to clean up while we kids put on heavy coats.

"Time to dig the spuds," Papa boomed.

We followed him to the garden, pulling on winter hats. I dreaded those nights.

Papa stood to the side of the first plant in a row and thrust a shovel in the ground about eight inches away from the stem. He stomped on the shovel with his right foot, plunging the blade deep into the soil. The edge of the shovel was sharp.

"Back in Ohio, I knew a kid who lost a finger when a shovel sliced it clean off," he said, chuckling. Papa had the same twisted sense of humor as his father, who also took delight in frightening children. "They fed the finger to the pigs."

I bit my lip to stop the taste of throw-up in my mouth. Tim and Eileen and I kneeled on the ground near his feet. He rocked the shovel back and forth in the soil. As soon as he lifted a clod of dirt, we grabbed potatoes and threw them in a bushel basket. I was afraid that if I put my hands near the ground too fast, the shovel would come down and chop off my fingers. And if I didn't pull the potatoes out quickly enough, my hands might end up buried. Papa made a game of us not losing fingers while we dug the spuds.

It was dark and damp by the time we went back to the house. My fingers were always numb. We watched Papa dump potatoes each night into a wooden bin he'd built in the coal cellar. We knew the potatoes had to reach the top before the harvest would be done, and the bin filled very, very slowly. We'd do the same thing the next night, and the next.

The fall that I was in fourth grade, I complained about having to dig potatoes. Papa told me that potatoes were in our genes and I should be grateful that we had a healthy crop. He said that the reason our Irish ancestors left Ireland for America was that a potato blight caused a huge famine in Ireland in the 1840s.

"People can live on potatoes," he declared. "They have all the vitamins you need. The Irish lived on potatoes for thousands of years."

"That's not true," I said.

He narrowed his eyes.

"In school we'd learned that Spanish Conquistadors discovered potatoes in the New World and took them back on ships. Europeans didn't start eating potatoes until the 18th century."

"I've warned you," he said.

I knew I should keep my mouth shut. And I couldn't help myself.

"But Gramp said the famine happened because the British oppressors were taking most of the crops and the meat from Ireland to England, and the peasants in Ireland had to live on potatoes and milk."

"They liked potatoes!" Papa said. He was getting angry. "They're good for you."

"They might have liked them, but it's not like they had any choice. And when the blight hit, the British kept taking all the other food, so the Irish starved."

"That's what I said!" Papa's voice was getting lower.

"But you said they ate them for thousands of years. And they only started eating them like a hundred years before…"

He slapped my mouth and chin.

"That will teach you to talk back."

7

NOT SAFE AT HOME

Papa joined the Berkshire County Association for Retarded Children shortly after Mary Jean went to Belchertown. Our family volunteered at the group's holiday parties in Pittsfield. Tim and I handed out cupcakes, Mom filled plastic cups with Hawaiian Punch, and Eileen wandered around looking for someone to play with while Papa talked to the other fathers.

Most of the families at the parties were "child at home" families. We were a "Belchertown" family, which carried a stigma. When Mom and Papa met new people, they always said exactly the same thing: "Our daughter is severely retarded, so we had no choice but to put her in Belchertown." They said "no choice" more loudly than the rest of the sentence.

Mom explained to me that severely retarded was not as bad as profoundly retarded, but worse than moderately retarded, trainable, or educable. As a child, I often wished that Mary Jean was "Mongoloid," the term used then for people with Down syndrome, because my parents said Mongoloids were gentle souls and not as retarded as Mary Jean. They could stay home.

After several years of volunteering, Papa was elected president of the Berkshire Association for Retarded Children. He also joined the Berkshire Mental Health Association and got elected president of that, too. He liked the control and prestige of these positions. It helped him prove to the outside world that he didn't just dump Mary Jean at Belchertown and forget about her. But he was often embroiled in political battles in his roles with both associations.

In 1964, two years after Mary Jean went to Belchertown, I heard Papa talking about a "special commission" after an Association for Retarded Children meeting. The legislation championed by President Kennedy before his death made federal dollars available to help states improve their facilities for the mentally retarded. To get ready to apply for funding, Massachusetts set up a special commission to look at the most pressing needs in the state's institutions. The commission's investigators reported that Belchertown, with a population of more than 1,500, was overcrowded by more than 20 percent and had a flagrant shortage of professionals. The commission called for more social services, psychologists and psychiatric personnel, doctors and nurses, teachers, rehabilitation specialists, and music, speech, and art therapists.

Papa supported the state's efforts to land federal funds to improve Belchertown, although he said Mary Jean was too retarded to really benefit from special therapies. Still, he could see that it might benefit other residents. But not everyone agreed that more funding for large institutions was the best way to improve care.

During the same time period, a few progressive psychologists began talking about "the normalization principle." Their research showed that putting retarded people in abusive environments caused under-functioning and additional impairment. The solution, they argued, was to close state institutions and develop community-based, supervised group homes.

Papa was vehemently opposed to group homes. He argued Belchertown was the best place to care for retarded people because they were better off living with their own kind. If they lived in a regular neighborhood, they might realize they were different from other people. Not Mary Jean, of course, because she was too severely retarded. But for other people, it might be a problem. It was better to keep everyone in Belchertown.

Other parents in Pittsfield disagreed. They felt sure they could find a neighborhood that would accept a group home, which would be staffed with round-the-clock caretakers. Kids could go to special education classes at public schools. When they grew up, they could be in a sheltered workshop. They'd be able to spend more time with their families.

But Papa, unskilled in finding points of common ground or seeking consensus, argued ferociously that this would never work. That was his way, and Papa's reputation as a difficult man grew.

While in college, he had proudly written to Mom about "sailing" into another student during a meeting about electing fraternity officers. "I straightened him out in front of the whole chapter. I told him it wasn't personal — it's just that I was right. I don't understand why he went away mad." In another letter, he gave this advice when Mom was having trouble with a colleague: "You should try to ignore her as much as possible while she is there, and don't worry about her when she isn't there. If I were in a situation like that, I would make as many cutting and ambiguous remarks as possible until I found her weakness and then shove the needle clear in and keep it there. She would be helpless as far as getting back at you."

He made many enemies in the Association for Retarded Children and the Mental Health Association as he fought attempts in the late 1960s to develop community-based homes as an alternative to Belchertown. Around the same time, he announced that Dr. Porter wouldn't be our pediatrician anymore.

When I asked why, Papa snapped, "I've told you not to ask so many questions!"

Later, I overheard Papa calling the doctor a turncoat. "I can't believe that Dr. Porter is questioning whether children like Mary Jean should be in Belchertown!" Papa told Mom with indignation.

Apparently after Mary Jean went to Belchertown, Dr. Porter reconsidered whether institutionalization was the only option for severely retarded children. After his death in 1988, I discovered he spent the final decades of his career advocating for community-based services for people with intellectual and developmental disabilities. He won awards and accolades from the Berkshire County Association for Retarded Citizens, the March of Dimes, and the state Department of Public Health. Dr. Porter helped set up the first Medicaid-funded day habilitation program in Pittsfield and served as the physician for the area's first intermediate care facility for people with complex disabilities and health problems.

I wonder how much different Mary Jean's life might have been if Dr. Porter had become a champion for community-based services just a few years earlier. He had the opportunity: the local Association for Retarded Children was organized in 1954, eight years before Mary Jean went to Belchertown. It was part of a national grassroots movement of parents lobbying for special education and living facilities that would help all people reach their potential. In 1973, the group changed its name to The Association for Retarded Citizens to be inclusive of adults, and then to The Arc in

1992 to rid itself of the pejorative word retardation. Today, The Arc continues to promote and protect the human rights of people with intellectual and developmental disabilities and actively supports their full inclusion and participation in the community throughout their lifetimes.

But Dr. Porter's awakening came too late, and my parents could not cope with any shift in the narrative set in motion by the advice they received in 1962. The layers of the story became their identities: anguished parents who had no choice but to institutionalize a defective child for the sake of their other children. In their minds, having made a mistake would be unforgivable.

Eileen and Mary Jean — A visit at home from Belchertown, house on Peck's Road, Pittsfield, about 1964

Although they continued to bring Mary Jean home for holiday overnight visits, Mom and Papa got migraines from the stress, and the visits weren't fun or satisfying. One Christmas in the house on Peck's Road, Mary Jean pulled the piano bench over and broke her toe. After Papa returned with Mary Jean from the hospital, he announced, "This is the last time we'll bring her here. She is not safe at home."

But she wasn't safe at Belchertown, either. At one visit, Mom and Papa were shocked to see Mary Jean in a cast. No one would tell them how her arm became fractured.

Papa, Mary Jean, and Mom —
Belchertown State School, mid-1960s

In December 1965, Burton Blatt, a professor at the University of Syracuse, and Fred Kaplan, a freelance photographer, visited Belchertown State School and four other institutions for the mentally retarded. Blatt was a nationally recognized leader in humanizing services for people with intellectual disabilities. Wearing a hidden camera on his belt,

Kaplan took photographs. Their findings were chronicled in a book: *Christmas in Purgatory: A Photographic Essay on Mental Retardation*.

"There is a hell on earth, and in America there is a special inferno. We were visitors there during Christmas, 1965," Blatt wrote. "The visits brought us to the depths of despair."

Photographs showed sleeping areas that were dirty and crowded, broken sinks and toilets, gaping holes in the walls and ceilings. Blatt described the fetid odor: "After a visit to a day room, we had to send our clothes to the dry cleaners to have the stench removed."

Residents who committed minor rule infractions were confined to solitary cells — without bed, toilet, or sink. Children's hands were tied and their legs bound. Blatt reported that one attendant said, "What can one do with those patients who do not conform? We must lock them up, or restrain them, or sedate them, or put fear in them."

I didn't become aware of the book until long after its publication. I don't know if my parents knew about it. I recognized the details from visits to Mary Jean: the shape of the wall tiles; eyes peering through the tiny window of a heavy wooden door; children clothed only in diapers sitting on a wooden bench or crouched naked on the floor. Our visits to Belchertown had almost normalized the horrors shown in the photos.

Blatt wrote: "There is a shame in America. Countless human beings are suffering needlessly. Countless more families of these unfortunate victims of society's irresponsibility are in anguish for they know, or suspect, the truth. Unwittingly, or unwillingly, they have been forced to institutionalize their loved one into a life of degradation and horror."

Blatt and Kaplan called for a national examination of programs, standards, personnel, budgets, philosophy, and objectives. "We now have a deep sorrow, one that will not abate until the American people are aware of — and do something about — the treatment of the severely mentally retarded in our state institutions." But despite legislative action and media attention, the residents of Belchertown remained well hidden from people living in the towns and cities of Massachusetts. Whole communities managed to abide by the advice of doctors to distraught parents: Forget that people with mental retardation were ever born.

Mary Jean, Mom, and Tim —
Belchertown State School, 1960s

The 1964 Massachusetts special commission's report did not result in meaningful changes at Belchertown. However, anticipation of federal funds led the Massachusetts legislature to pass the Comprehensive Mental Health and Retardation Services Act in 1966, which directed the Department of Mental Retardation to deinstitutionalize and decentralize services. The department appointed Dr. Philip Wakstein as the first regional administrator for the department's western Massachusetts office. Community advocates started or ramped up nonprofit agencies to provide support and services for people with disabilities.

My parents' fear that Belchertown might close intensified when I was ten and Mom found herself unexpectedly pregnant.

"We didn't plan to have another baby," I overhead Mom telling a friend, "but it will be a welcomed child. Thank goodness Mary Jean is in Belchertown, though. We'd never be able to manage a bigger family if she was still at home."

Mom and Papa must have been anxious at the prospect of another retarded child, but they never discussed it in front of us. We heard them worry about Belchertown closing, and they talked a lot about household expenses. They'd come to depend on the money Mom earned as a substitute teacher, and a new baby meant she wouldn't be able to work for a while. But I was scared the baby might be retarded. Mom and Papa seemed unaware that their children were apprehensive about bad things that might happen.

And bad things did happen. During fifth grade, I sometimes went to my neighbor Mary Ann's house after school. She'd ask me to help with hard homework because schoolwork came easily to me. I liked being at Mary Ann's. Her parents were a lot more relaxed than mine. Her Mom deep-fried Polish cookies called angel wings for us.

Her cute older brother, Walter, was a freshman at Berkshire Community College. One Sunday morning, we heard on the radio that Walter had been killed in a car crash on Hancock Road. Mom and Papa took me to the wake to pay our respects. Mary Ann didn't seem to recognize me when I said I was very sorry and would pray for her family. Walter lay in an open casket, his head swollen to a grotesque size and his face caked thick with makeup. I closed my eyes when I kneeled on a white cushion next to the casket to say a quick "Glory Be to the Father," but couldn't help peeping through the slits of my eyelids.

"That was such bad taste," Papa said on the ride home. "What were they thinking to have an open casket when he was so mangled? But what do you expect of Polacks?" Mom, as usual, was silent. No one noticed my hands were trembling. The trauma of seeing Walter in the casket was compounded by my indignation that Papa used a degrading slur.

I woke up crying that night after dreaming of Walter's head going through the windshield as he hit the tree. Papa yelled at me to quiet down. In the absence of any comforting from my parents, my anxiety about life's dangers grew.

In early June 1966, my brother Paul Michael was born. Excited about being a big sister again, but still worried that he might be retarded, I stayed home from fifth grade the day that Mom was going to leave the hospital. Nana dropped Aunt El at our house in the morning. It was a beautiful day, with a cloudless blue sky and a balmy temperature. Aunt El and I sat in folding lawn chairs near the driveway, admiring the pink peonies in the flower garden as we waited for Papa's car to appear.

"Why are there always ants on peonies?" I wondered aloud, walking over to look more closely at the blossoms.

Aunt El grunted. I turned around. One of her eyes was wide open. The other was nearly shut, and that side of her face drooped. She grunted again.

"Aunt El," I said, grabbing her shoulders. "What's wrong?"

I'd read every children's chapter book about nursing that I could get my hands on — the entire Cherry Ames and Sue Barton series — plus the Red Cross First Aid Manual. Aunt El was in her late seventies, and I knew something was seriously awry. I could hear voices next door and yelled for help, but my voice didn't carry. I was afraid Aunt El would fall out of her chair, so I eased her to the ground, struggling to control her heavy body with my thin arms. I ran into the house. The inside front cover of the phone book had a number for an ambulance. I dialed, said that an elderly woman was very ill, and asked them to come as quickly as possible.

Then I looked up the number for Pittsfield General Hospital. When the operator answered I told her to connect me with the maternity ward.

"I can't do that," she said. "Our policy is . . . "

"It's an emergency," I said forcefully. "If you don't connect me, we will have a real problem. It could be a matter of life and death."

She put me on hold. When another voice came on the line, I gave my name and said that Mr. Paul Flanagan had to come home immediately to deal with an emergency. As I ran back through the kitchen, I grabbed a towel and went outside to stay with Aunt El. The day was getting hot and Aunt El was no longer in the shade. I draped the towel over her face to try to keep her cool.

When Papa arrived, he yelled to the men next door and soon they were helping Papa move Aunt El inside to the living room couch. The ambulance had not yet arrived. I wondered if maybe the Kents had been right years earlier when they put Papa in their car to take him to the hospital instead of waiting for an ambulance.

"I left your mother sitting at the nurse's station with the baby in her arms," Papa said. "You stay with Aunt El while I go back to get her."

I was scared. I wet a washcloth with cool water and held it against Aunt El's pale forehead. She drifted in and out of consciousness. Each time a truck drove by, I ran to the window thinking it would be the ambulance. Finally, I heard a car in the driveway. Mom walked in holding the baby in her arms, Papa's hand cradling her elbow.

"Aunt El, this is Paul Michael," Mom said. "Isn't he beautiful?"

"I don't know anything about that baby!" Aunt El said indignantly, emphasizing the word "anything." Up to that point, she had only grunted or moaned. I was relieved she could talk.

"Of course, you do," Mom said. "This is my new baby. Paul, like his father."

"Harrumph," Aunt El said.

The ambulance arrived then. There was a lot of commotion as two men strapped Aunt El to a stretcher. Papa went to the kitchen to mix formula for Paul's bottle, and Mom slumped in an arm chair. Nana never made it back to our house that day. She went straight to the hospital to check on Aunt El, who'd been diagnosed with a stroke. Aunt El made a remarkable recovery and was back home a few days later.

"You're quite the girl, Sherry," Gramp said the next time he stopped by our house. "That was quick thinking to take such good care of Eleanor. You have a good head on your shoulders."

His eyes shone. I smiled at him, proud that I'd been useful.

For the next few weeks, Mom was gloomy, struggling to get through each day. She'd prop Paul in the bassinette and roll a receiving blanket to hold his bottle in place. I'd scoop him up and cuddle him as he drank the formula. She'd put him in the plastic bathtub and soap and rinse his body in less than a minute. I'd offer to watch him and gave him toys to splash in the water. I took him for walks in the baby buggy and spread out a blanket on the lawn so that he could watch the birds and clouds. At eleven years old, I'd outgrown dolls and was thrilled to have a real baby to lavish with affection.

After several weeks of increasingly lethargic behavior, Mom didn't get up one morning and was still in bed when Papa came home from work. Her doctor made a house call that evening and spent almost an hour with Mom and Papa in their bedroom. I listened outside the closed door but couldn't make out what they were saying.

"Your mother needs to go to the hospital," Papa said when he emerged. "She has high blood pressure. Call your grandmother. You watch the kids until she gets here."

Papa led Mom to the car. She was in the hospital for a week. I assumed she was at Pittsfield General, where the new baby was born, but I overheard Papa say "Brattleboro" during a phone call, and it stuck in my head. Later I learned that there was a private psychiatric hospital in Brattleboro, Vermont, about an hour-and-a-half drive from Pittsfield. Now I assume that she was being treated for postpartum depression, but Mom and Papa never talked about it. Throughout their lives, no matter how much pressure they were under, they constructed a façade of well-being. They never spoke about the tangle of mental health problems that ensnared them both.

At the time, though, I believed the high blood pressure story, and I did my best to take care of the baby, the younger kids, and the house. I didn't want Mom to worry. It still haunted me that I hadn't been able to keep Mary Jean safe. I was determined that nothing bad would happen to my family again.

8
MOUTHING OFF

Papa's anger intensified after Mom came home from the hospital, even though we followed his instructions and were especially quiet and helpful. Why did she take so many naps, he snapped, and why did she let the house fall apart? He came home livid from work one day: once again, he didn't get a raise because his boss was out to get him. Mary Jean continued to suffer unexplained injuries, and there was more talk about moving people from Belchertown to their home communities. Papa cleaned his gardening tools obsessively that summer and tinkered endlessly with his huge lawnmower.

It was a pattern he'd described to Mom in a letter while they were in college: "I get blue, and then I get angry with myself and the world in general and go into a frenzy of activity in an attempt to get myself back on equilibrium. I pray to the Virgin Mary to intercede on my behalf. No one will ever convince me that prayer and faith cannot overcome almost all obstacles if it is for the good of the individual to have their desires." His desire was for a calm home and a happy wife. But we were a family of four young kids, with all the chaos that implied, another child who was institutionalized, and a depressed, barely functional wife.

One Saturday morning, Papa squatted in the garage, swearing as he banged a wrench against the lawnmower's engine. As quietly as I could, I tried to scoot past him toward the rickety wooden stairs to the hayloft, looking forward to settling in with a book.

"Where do you think you're going?" Papa asked.

"To the hayloft," I mumbled.

"Go in the house and help your mother."

I objected. I'd worked all morning and recited to him the list of chores I'd already done: cleaning the kitchen, vacuuming, doing a load of wash.

Papa was unmoved, and our argument escalated.

"I said go in the house! The laundry will need folding. All you ever do is sit on your fanny reading books. You read too damn many books. They can put dangerous ideas in your head. Ideas you can never get out of your head."

I turned my face up to him. At age eleven, I'd reached my full adult height — four feet, eleven inches — but I weighed less than sixty pounds. I tucked the copy of James Michener's *Hawaii* that I'd checked out of the library under my arm.

"Ideas are not dangerous!" I shouted.

His face darkened. Purple blood vessels pushed through the skin of his forehead. I'd never before seen such intense fury in his eyes. My muscles tightened in fright.

"You will NOT mouth off to me. I'll show you, you little bitch."

Don't breathe, I told myself. My mother's words six years earlier roared in my ears: any time there's a fire, cut off the oxygen!

His brutal violence toward me that day extinguished my love for him, although he never again touched me in anger. In the months and years that followed, he alternated between ire and affection toward all his children, but I was unable to trust his attempts to show caring. I felt unsafe in his presence, even when he was an old man.

I lost the hayloft as my reading refuge. I didn't want to go near it. Unless I was helping with the housework or taking care of the baby, I stayed in my room. It was hard to fall asleep at night. I got headaches almost every day. When I was with Papa, I tried to talk exactly the right amount — enough so that he wouldn't get mad at me for being sullen but not so much that he could accuse me of mouthing off. He'd taught me a horrible lesson about speaking my mind.

Tending my brother Paul helped mitigate my anxiety. I rushed home from school each day to take care of him. He was a happy, bright, engaged baby. His nursery was a small room upstairs that once had been used as a den. It had ugly dark brown wallpaper, and lime green paint on the woodwork and built-in bookcase.

When we first moved to Peck's Road, I had a pretty bedroom with floral wallpaper and sheer white curtains to myself, and Eileen was stuck in the brown room. After Paul's birth she moved in with me, and we bickered about messiness and encroaching on each other's space.

After one fight with Eileen, I announced I was moving in with Paul. My parents didn't say no, so I dragged my bed and dresser down the hall and squeezed them in next to his crib. I assumed that Eileen would be glad to have the nice big bedroom to herself so she could be loud and disorganized. Years later, I discovered that she had been thrilled to move in with her big sister, hoping to be part of the older kids' activities. My rejection of a shared room became another layer in Eileen's feeling that she didn't hold an important place in the family. And I couldn't share with her what it meant to me to wake each morning to Paul's big blue eyes and gleeful squeal when he saw me. His smile became my reason for living.

When it was time to visit Mary Jean, I often faked a sore throat or claimed that I had a lot of homework so that I could stay with Nana and Gramp. I did everything I could to avoid spending time with my father, and I felt completely relaxed and sheltered in the house we called Fifty-Two. I'd bring along the notes about our family history that I'd started taking as a seven-year-old, and Gramp would tell me more stories about his grandparents and sisters. Although I had no appetite at home, I craved the rich macaroni and cheese Nana made for me, and the snacks of cream cheese on Ritz crackers and Lipton's onion dip with State Line potato chips. I didn't mind the small chores that Nana gave to me — polishing the Tiffany silver flatware that she received as a wedding gift and using Windex to clean the windows of the small sunroom that overlooked the side yard.

Just after Easter the year I was in sixth grade, Papa said he'd made a big decision about my future. He had often talked about the importance of a Catholic education. Public schools, he'd always asserted, didn't have a foundation in truth. His announcement that he and Mom had decided that the public schools did a better job educating kids in junior and senior high was a shock. After they told Sister Superior to transfer my records to North Junior High School, the nuns started a campaign to get me to change my mind. Sister Lucia Gabriel, the seventh-grade teacher, led the charge. "North is a haven for heathens," she intoned. "You'll be raped in the hallways." I was shocked. Popular magazines like *Time* and *Newsweek* were publishing articles about the bourgeoning sexual revolution, but I didn't expect a nun to use such an explicit term.

I wasn't scared of North. I hated St. Charles, and I welcomed a fresh start. Though I was determined to make friends at this school, people didn't seem to like me. But then, I didn't like myself very much, either. I was angry all the time — angry when my grades sometimes dropped from A-plus to just plain A, angry that I couldn't say what I wanted to say at home without getting hurt. Angry that, even though Papa said I acted too smart, I wasn't good enough or strong enough or smart enough to fix all the things wrong in my family. Trying to fake cheerfulness made things worse. I remember a girl saying to me, "Why do you smile all the time? It's creepy. You smile even when there's nothing to smile about."

Despite my social awkwardness, I performed well at North, acing my classwork and writing for the school newspaper, *The Northern Light*. I focused on issues like the injustice of boys being able to wear jeans but girls weren't allowed to. I wrote about the poisonous chemicals that GE was spewing into a small nearby lake. The school reversed its policy on jeans, although some teachers protested that the school was becoming infested with women's libbers. But my article questioning why Silver Lake didn't freeze in the winter went unnoticed, except for Papa, who got angry. He claimed that there was nothing dangerous about the waste that GE dumped in the lake.

"The water dilutes the compounds," he said. "There's absolutely no danger."

He would change his mind. He became convinced that his exposure to polychlorinated biphenyls, or PCBs, when he worked with transformers at GE was the source of the health problems that plagued him in the last decades of his life.

9

ARE YOU LONESOME TONIGHT?

Throughout my childhood, I could be found at least once a week at the Berkshire Athenaeum, Pittsfield's public library, a beautiful stone building in the center of town. When I was twelve, a book called *The Siege* was displayed on the Local Authors table near the front desk. A small sign written in calligraphy said, "By Clara Claiborne Park, Williamstown." I knew Berkshire County had been home to famous authors like Herman Melville, Nathaniel Hawthorne, Henry Wadsworth Longfellow, Edith Wharton, and more, but it hadn't occurred to me that real writers still lived in the area. I'd decided by then that, in addition to being a nurse, I wanted to be a writer when I grew up. I was curious about Clara Claiborne Park.

I opened the book. On the first page, Clara wrote, "We are a bookish family." I remember thinking how wonderful that family must be. Mom still had her English literature books from college, and we had a Collier's Encyclopedia, but Papa disapproved of most books. He warned over and over again that books were full of dangerous ideas you could never get out of your head.

On the second page, Clara said that her young daughter was slow to talk: "Out of nowhere words appear. And into nowhere they disappear." That sounded like Mary Jean.

I desperately wanted to understand what was wrong with my younger sister. How did she get that way? And what would happen as she grew older? Every time I asked, my parents replied: "We don't know. There's no way we'll ever know."

The Park family lived in a beautiful college town twenty miles north of Pittsfield. Clara and her husband, David, were professors. He taught physics at Williams College, and when she was not at home raising children, she taught English at a college over the mountain in New York state. Their daughter Jessy, called Elly in early editions of the book to protect her privacy, was six months older than Mary Jean.

As an infant and toddler, Jessy was slow to walk and spoke only isolated words. She did not point to objects or seek attention. The Parks concluded that Jessy was mentally retarded and when they felt the time had come to "press for certainty" about their child's condition, they connected with a nationally known pediatrician knowledgeable about the most recent developments in mental and physical illness. When she was almost three years old, Jessy, like Mary Jean, was evaluated at Boston Children's Hospital. Unlike Mary Jean, Jessy was given the diagnosis of autism.

I don't know if doctors in Boston talked to my parents about autism. The condition is widely known today — one in fifty-nine children in the United States have been diagnosed on the autism spectrum, a continuum of brain disorders with a complex array of symptoms. But when Jessy and Mary Jean were toddlers in the early 1960s, it was a relatively new and a most unwelcome diagnosis. Back then, pediatricians and child psychiatrists thought that autism was a form of schizophrenia caused by cold, detached "refrigerator mothers" who withheld affection from their children. If autism had been broached in

Boston, my parents likely would have rejected the diagnosis. Mental retardation, while heartbreaking, was far more socially acceptable than autism.

Today, the American Psychiatric Association's Diagnostic and Statistical Manual of Mental Disorders, a manual known as the DSM-V, defines a range of conditions as Autism Spectrum Disorder or ASD. People with ASD always have restricted, repetitive patterns of behavior, interests, or activities, but differ greatly in how they are affected by the condition. Deficits in social communication and interactions are sometimes accompanied by intellectual disabilities. Some people with ASD are highly functional and respond well to interventions that help them learn social skills and verbal communication. Others have excellent communication skills but experience problems with the basics of getting through a day. Some have significant challenges in communicating and interacting with others, and some are completely nonverbal. It's not unusual for people on the spectrum to have complex medical problems, too.

The siege that gave Clara Claiborne Park's book its title was the decision to "use every stratagem we could invent to assail her fortress." When Jessy was diagnosed, little was understood about autism. The doctors in Boston recommended that Clara and David continue doing what they'd been doing and give Jessy affection. In addition to affection, the Parks came up with a host of interventions to help Jessy connect with the world.

When describing the challenges of raising Jessy, Clara related the story of her grandmother keeping a severely retarded child — Clara's uncle — at home for years and then putting him in an institution — "To spare the family, I suppose, but I think also to spare herself. She couldn't bear it."

When I read those words, anger flared. "Just like Mom and Papa spared themselves," I muttered. "They couldn't bear it."

Clara flooded Jessy with attention and love. David provided consistent support to his wife and their other children. They were the parents I wished I had. Clara was a fighter. David was kind. My mother was depressed. My father was angry. They said sending Mary Jean away was to make life better for their other children, but it wasn't true. Putting Mary Jean in Belchertown didn't make things better for us. Our lives were still filled with stress and rage. They sent Mary Jean away because Mom didn't have the stamina to care for her, and Papa wanted her dead.

I was Mary Jean's older sister, and I was furious I hadn't figured out a way to bring order to the chaos of our lives. As a preteen, I had no empathy for my parents' pain or the limits of their experiences and abilities, although scant resources existed in the 1960s for parents to learn how to raise a child with developmental disabilities. I also lacked compassion for myself, for the heartache I'd experienced. My heart was fully with Mary Jean and her abandonment, her injuries, her trauma. Clara became my mythic heroine, a warrior. I could not distinguish between Clara's ability to mount a siege upon a passive, nearly immobile child, and my mother, who felt under siege by a child wracked with seizures — terrified, shrieking, violent.

Jessy and Mary Jean had different issues, but after reading *The Siege,* I wondered if Mary Jean might have both autism and retardation. She had gained and then lost vocabulary as a toddler. She repeated words she heard but didn't use them with any purpose. She ate a small number of foods and then refused to eat at all. Her limbs were stiff and spastic. I remembered her vacant eyes as a baby, the hours she spent turning the rubber doll over and over in her hands. She expressed anger but didn't connect with people verbally or emotionally. I waited anxiously after asking Mom to read *The Siege,* but when we talked about the book, she said I was being silly to compare Mary Jean and Jessy. Mary Jean was severely retarded, and nothing could be done. Once again, denial kept her from considering ways that Mary Jean's life might be improved.

Jessy attended a small private preschool and then a class for the educable retarded at the local public school. Her passivity as a toddler changed to hyperactivity. Exercises in visual perception and arithmetic, which were easy for Jessy to complete, were secondary to more difficult lessons about greeting others, responding to an overture, and listening with patience to a classmate.

The Siege concluded six-and-a-half years after the start of the Parks' assault on Jessy's fortress. Clara described Jessy as occasionally frustrated and anxious at home, but "in the main gay, active, full of cheerful noises and cheerful words. But if you were to watch her outside, you would see something very different." Jessy couldn't talk or play in the same way as neighborhood children. She did not join them in riding bikes, pulling wagons, snow fights, or hide-and-seek. Instead, "she swings and swings, or eats snow, or plays with sand as of old, dribbling it from a spoon." Children avoided conversations with Jessy unless Clara was there to interpret her speech and behavior.

How might Mary Jean's life have been different, I wondered, if someone had taught her to connect with others when she was small, and taken the time to interpret her speech and behavior? My trust in my parents' conviction that nothing could be done for Mary Jean evaporated after I read *The Siege*, and they rebuffed my questions.

Mom and Papa continued their biweekly visits to Belchertown. Although I sometimes invented excuses so I could spend the day with Nana and Gramp, most of the time I went. Papa said we had an obligation to go because we were her family, and we weren't the kind of people who would abandon a child.

As Mary Jean grew, her feet got worse. She limped and flinched in pain. Twice a year we went to a special shop in the town of Ware to buy expensive orthopedic shoes that a doctor said she should wear all the time. But the Belchertown staff didn't keep track of the shoes. She'd wear someone else's dirty white sneakers one week, and huge navy-blue loafers a few weeks later. One ankle was so weak that the bottom of her foot rolled inward; she walked on her ankle instead of her foot. She had an operation to fix the muscles and tendons. Recovery from the surgery was dreadful. Mary Jean lay in a hospital bed in the Belchertown infirmary for months.

Once she could walk again, Papa wrote to the school's superintendent, Dr. Bowser, demanding that attendants put Mary Jean in her orthopedic shoes every morning. But her shoes and clothes were constantly disappearing. Nana bought special things for Mary Jean — corduroy pants with elastic waistbands, pretty floral turtlenecks, cardigan sweaters, a warm parka. Buying gifts was Nana's way to feel connected to Mary Jean. Nana and Gramp didn't visit because Mom said it would be too upsetting. After a while, Mom told Nana to stop the gifts. We never saw Mary Jean wearing her own clothes.

One day an attendant, new to Belchertown, whispered to Mom that some staff members stole the gifts intended for residents, and gave them to their own family and friends. Papa said we shouldn't report this or complain, because staff might treat Mary Jean badly, but I didn't see how the care could get any worse. Residents often sat in the dayrooms naked. Mom talked wistfully about expensive private facilities like the one Pearl Buck chose for her daughter and supported with large financial gifts. She was envious and angry that our family did not have the wealth to put Mary Jean in a better place than Belchertown, but she didn't want to bring her home, either.

During one of our visits when Mary Jean was about ten, the sisters and brothers of retarded children were allowed to ride on a delightful carousel that the institution's Friends Association operated near the administration building. The carved wooden horses had beautiful roses around their necks and brightly colored saddles and bridles. Mary Jean screamed when we tried to coax her toward the carousel.

"The movement and the music are probably too much stimulation," Papa said. "I'll take her for a walk." He took her hand, and they walked away down Front Street.

I sat on a big white horse with a blue saddle, wondering if at fourteen I was too old, but still wanting a ride. The usual merry-go-round music played for a while and then we circled to the beat of Elvis Presley singing *Are You Lonesome Tonight?* and *Don't Be Cruel.* I couldn't get the songs out of my head on the long drive home.

As Mary Jean's physical and emotional health continued to deteriorate, tending to the big garden and yard on Peck's Road no longer helped Papa stay calm. Mom complained that Nana was right — we did live in a seedy part of town. Her dream was to live on one of the parkways, quiet streets with narrow bands of grass and shrubs down the center. GE managers lived on the parkways, Mom said with envy, but Papa had little hope of a promotion. His education, skills, and quick temper did not make advancement at GE likely.

During the spring of eighth grade, Papa told us over dinner one night that we would be moving, not to a house on a parkway but to Mountain Drive, a relatively new development on the outskirts of town.

"It's a great house," Papa said. "Very spacious. You'll all have your own rooms. Sharon and Tim will transfer to South Junior High. And the elementary school for Eileen — and Paul, when he's bigger — will have a much better element."

That was his way of telling us, yet again, that we were better than the kids in our Peck's Road neighborhood. He worried about our exposure to what he called "unsavory influences."

I was devastated. I'd been elected editor of the school paper at North and another transfer sounded unbearable. But I knew better than to say anything right away. I had to wait for the right moment to make my case. A few weeks later, the moment came.

"It came through," he told Mom when he came in the door after work. "I got the raise!"

He took Mom in his arms and gave her a long kiss on the lips, then squeezed her butt.

"Paul," she said, drawing out his name. She was flustered and happy. "Not now. And that's great! Sharon, set the table."

Papa pulled a bottle of Old Grand-Dad from a high kitchen shelf.

"This calls for a drink," he said, taking two lowball glasses from another cabinet and pulling open the freezer for ice.

Now was the time.

"Congratulations, Papa," I said.

He beamed.

"I was thinking," I said. "You know how I need to transfer to South? Well, I was just wondering if maybe I could get a ride with you when you go to work, and walk the rest of the way to North, and just stay there for another year."

And with that, I shut up. I didn't mention how important it was to be editor of the paper, or how hard it had been to change schools so many times. I didn't say anything that he could argue with.

"That could work," he said. He was eyeing Mom and squeezed her butt again.

"Great, then it's settled!" I replied.

He did not renege. Every morning of ninth grade, I was ready early so that I wouldn't make him late, and I'd climb in the front seat of his green VW bug. He dropped me off on Tyler Street or, if he was in a good mood, he drove me all the way to the school. I think he felt guilty for hurting me so horribly that day near the hayloft stairs, and this was a way to make himself feel better. He could tell himself he was a good father who went out of his way to accommodate his daughter's wishes.

Still, he ruled with an iron fist. I knew a mini-skirt or go-go boots would be out of the question, but I used my babysitting money to buy fishnet stockings at Newberry's five and dime one Saturday. I carefully unrolled them onto my matchstick legs Monday morning, thrilled with my unprecedented foray into dressing like the cool kids.

"You look like a hooker," Papa snapped when I walked into the kitchen. "Get those things off you. And I want to see them in this garbage can!"

Mom bit her lower lip and said nothing.

10

THE TRAGEDY OF BELCHERTOWN

Mary Jean will never be able to tell us what she experienced during her years at Belchertown. But for several years, she lived in the same building as a highly intelligent, profoundly disabled girl who eventually found a way let the world know what was going on. Ruth Sienkiewicz-Mercer told her story in a remarkable memoir, *I Raise My Eyes to Say Yes.*

Ruth entered Belchertown at the same time as Mary Jean, in the spring of 1962. Mary Jean was three and Ruth, almost twelve. In early infancy, Ruth fell ill with a severe infection, probably encephalitis. Consequently, she developed cerebral palsy — the only parts of her body that functioned normally were her eyes, ears, nose, and digestive system. Her vocal cords could produce only ten distinct sounds, not nearly enough to speak.

Ruth's parents, with the help of extended family, cared for her at home for several years. As her needs increased, her parents enrolled her in Crotched Mountain, an excellent, expensive rehabilitation facility in New Hampshire. A few years later, the family's financial downturn forced them to withdraw Ruth from Crotched Mountain. Unable to care for her at home, her parents took her to Belchertown.

Ruth was able to communicate through facial expressions. However, the staff doctor who examined Ruth upon admission ignored, or perhaps didn't understand, her parents' explanation about the meaning of her facial signals. Most doctors at Belchertown were born and trained outside the United States, and limited English-language skills often made conversations with families difficult.

After a brief evaluation, the doctor wrote "imbecile" in Ruth's record, which should have meant she could be trained based on the definition still used by Belchertown staff. But because no one realized that she spoke with her face, staff believed that Ruth understood nothing. She spent the next eight years completely unable to communicate her needs. Her parents visited often, but because she could not form words, she had no way to let them know how bad things were. At one point, she was in agony with a broken leg for three days before a high fever got the staff's attention. She was finally taken to a hospital for treatment.

A turning point came in 1969 when graduate students of a nearby university introduced a new approach to Belchertown residents called augmentative communication. Nonverbal people learned to "talk" by pointing to pictures glued to a wooden board. Ruth directed an assistant to a letter or picture with her eyes and responding to verbal queries with a "yes" or "no" facial expression. Mary Jean participated in the same program, although my parents dismissed its usefulness.

"That's completely ridiculous," Papa declared when a ward attendant said Mary Jean had used a picture board to say she was thirsty. "Her brain is way too damaged. The eggheads from U Mass are just imagining things."

We now know that interventions for children with developmental delays, especially at an early age, are highly effective. My parents' resistance to augmentative communication came both from guilt that they'd institutionalized Mary Jean and fear that she might have to live with us if officials decided that she wasn't retarded enough to need Belchertown. Barely able to manage our brief visits with her, they were terrified at the prospect of being responsible for Mary Jean's daily care.

The communication program gave Ruth a voice. She wrote her memoir with help from Steven Kaplan, who provided individualized educational and socialization training for Ruth after she left Belchertown in 1978. Ruth described the pain, despair, hope, and love she experienced. And she documented — in excruciating detail — the neglect and abuse endured by Belchertown residents while she was there.

When I saw photos of Ruth in the memoir, I remembered her clenched hands, thin arms, and long, long legs from my visits to Mary Jean.

Ruth's braces and wheelchair were taken away when she entered Belchertown. She never again saw them, or her clothes, or her beloved doll, Gretl. She had been toilet trained and needed only physical assistance to use the bathroom, yet she was diapered. During her first week at Belchertown, Ruth lay on her back, alone in a room, because staff didn't want her to bring in any communicable diseases.

She wrote about how frightening that time was: "Lying in that bed…I became aware of very strange noises coming through the walls and ceiling. These noises — groaning, moaning, screaming — were being made by people, that much I could tell. But I couldn't imagine what kind of people were making them. The possibilities scared me, and I tried to block the noises out."

She also described the horrors of eating, both the food and the process of eating. Her mother had always fed her, cutting her food into small pieces so she could eat slowly. She wrote, "At Belchertown the attendants shoved gobs of food into my mouth and expected me to swallow them in big gulps while I was flat on my back, not even propped up in a sitting position. The food was awful, the worst I had ever tasted. They fed me either boiled vegetables or steamed meat, ground into a tasteless pulp."

When Ruth choked on her food, the attendants became angry. "They thought I was being uncooperative," she wrote.

When she was finally taken to a ward, her relief at being with other people was quickly subsumed by the conditions she found: "The odor was sickening, the air was stale, and the atmosphere was lifeless." She said the ward "seemed a human wasteland. It presented a staggering array of crippled bodies and damaged minds, a living picture of pain and madness."

Ruth described a girl who "liked to stick her hands into her diapers, extract her own excrement, and smear it all over herself, her bed, and whatever else she could reach," something I remembered seeing during my first visit to Mary Jean. That girl and others who did the same were put in straitjackets. Ruth described head bangers who were put in boxing gloves and hockey helmets to prevent them from seriously hurting themselves.

Ruth's descriptions matched what I'd seen glimpsing into the dayrooms and wards of Belchertown. I had other memories, too. The infirmary had long horizontal bricks in different shades of tan and beige. The window frames were painted peppermint green in some parts of the building and sky blue in others. One day I counted the panes of the huge windows — five panes across and six panes high. Thirty pieces of glass for each window, but the windows were too clouded with dirt for residents to look outside.

In 1968, the American Association of Mental Deficiency released a follow-up report about Belchertown State School. A new dormitory had been completed and some residents had transferred to other institutions, but Belchertown was still seriously overcrowded and understaffed. Conditions dangerously impaired the care of residents, investigators said, "particularly the severely and profoundly retarded."

Mary Jean, Mom, and Paul —
Town Common, Belchertown, about 1969

Tim, Mary Jean, and Mom —
Town Common, Belchertown, about 1969

State officials took this report seriously, probably because federal dollars were on the table. The state Assistant Commissioner for Mental Retardation, William Fraenkel, visited Belchertown for twenty-four hours in 1969 to learn about the situation first hand. He described seeing nude women in Building A eating food from a single metal bowl. Feces coated the walls and floors. Residents shoved and hit each other, screamed, and ripped off their clothes. A partially nude woman, restrained with cotton tape to a pole, walked in an endless circle, her feet bare.

In Building K, forty men classified as severe-profound were kept naked at all times. An attendant explained, "It is easier to keep them clean this way. . . all we do is scrub them down after meal time in the shower room. What a mess it would be if they had their clothes on and a lot more work for us."

Reports issued in the late 1960s about conditions at Belchertown had not garnered much public attention. That changed in 1970 when the *Springfield Republican* and *Springfield Union*, sister newspapers in central Massachusetts, ran a six-part series titled "The Tragedy of Belchertown." Each article appeared as a front-page lead story, upstaging headlines such as "Pentagon Bids Nixon Keep Draft" and "Wounded Pilot Lands Jet After Gunman Kills Copilot."

Investigative reporter James M. Shanks wrote that the institution resembled a 19th century insane asylum more than a so-called residential school. The sterile environment encouraged insanity as an escape from stark reality. His writing style was sensational, but he backed up allegations with facts and photographs.

Shanks quoted Dr. Philip Wakstein, Regional Director of Mental Retardation for the Department of Mental Health: "Being placed in Belchertown from early childhood almost guarantees a child will never grow into a person capable of limited self-care."

During the day, only three attendants staffed Nursery II, the building where Mary Jean and thirty-three other severely retarded children lived. Beds were placed end to end in a sea of child-sized bunks. The day rooms, where children spent most of their time, were disgraceful.

Shanks wrote, "There is a large room with a terrazzo floor which easily can injure a young head or knee. Hard wooden benches, replicas of prison-made seats in the adult buildings, ring the walls. Prison-made benches are much cheaper than soft little chairs. The television set is in a glass and steel cage, along with a couple of old auto tires and some empty plastic bottles for the kids to play with."

Dr. Gunmar Dybwad, a respected expert and consultant to the President's Committee on Mental Retardation, was aghast at Belchertown's conditions, especially the dehumanization. He told Shanks: "There is one basic principle which should be followed in dealing with the retarded, or the mentally ill, or the handicapped. That is normalization. The retarded person should live in as normal a condition as circumstances will allow. He should not live in an institution which is totally alien to everyday living, which strips his very humanity from him."

Belchertown was lacking the reforms happening in other places, Shanks wrote, where there were facilities for diagnosing and treating retardation, day care, workshops and vocational training, and group homes. "None of these programs are new or innovative. Other states have them in operation, successfully, at a savings of tax dollars."

A TV station in Hartford, Connecticut aired a one-hour documentary about Belchertown called *They Need Love, They Get Angry, They Bleed*. When I learned about the film while doing research on Belchertown many years later, it was hard to watch. Attendants restrained residents' arms and legs and used drugs to keep them quiet. Experts described how Belchertown's lack of privacy had a rapid, negative impact.

Residents regressed quickly after living in the institution. As scene followed horrifying scene, I felt sick to my stomach, thinking yes, that is what I remember. Mary Jean's passivity, her slack jaw, her vacant eyes were caused by heavy sedation.

A fellow member of the Association for Retarded Children called my father about the "Tragedy of Belchertown" series, and Papa found copies.

"My God," Papa said when he came home and told Mom about the stories. "How could the editor let this be published? Don't they understand how many people they'll hurt?"

He slammed his fist on the kitchen counter. Mom opened the freezer to get ice cubes for bourbon and water.

A lot of people knew they had a daughter at Belchertown. My parents were fully aware of the filth and abuse, but they had a deep fear that if the problems came to light, they might be judged by people at church, by our neighbors, and by Papa's co-workers at GE for confining Mary Jean to such an appalling institution. They worried people would think, or even say out loud, "What kind of parent would leave their child in a place like that?"

Papa was protective of the public persona he had crafted. He did not want people to think he put his child in an institution and forgot about her, even though that's exactly what our parish priest and experts of the day had told him to do. My parents told themselves that committing Mary Jean to Belchertown left her in the hands of people with adequate training to care for her.

Even deeper was their fear that the state would close Belchertown. What would happen to Mary Jean? Would they have to bring her home? They had not been able to cope and keep her safe at home for even a weekend or holiday. They could barely handle her on short car rides when we visited.

Late in their lives, Mom and Papa talked about the emotions that had tormented them.

"I was so ashamed," Papa said. "You know the bridge on the Mass Pike in Russell, the one over the river and the valley? I thought how much better off Mary Jean would be if she dropped over. That was awful. Just the fact that the thought came into my mind, I was so ashamed of myself."

Mom said, "When I first became fully aware of the abuse Mary Jean suffered at Belchertown, my whole being rose up in revolt and horror. I had closed my eyes to what should have been obvious. I believe I had taken the easy way out in placing Mary Jean."

11

OUT OF THEIR MISERY

Scores of families and public officials used the "Tragedy of Belchertown" exposé to demand reforms with even louder voices than before. In 1970, the state legislature appointed a Joint Commission to investigate conditions at Belchertown State School and Monson State Hospital, a mental hospital accused of similar abuses. Along with state senators and representatives, two citizens were appointed to the Commission, including Benjamin Ricci, president of the Belchertown State School Friends Association.

A group of parents and relatives of Belchertown residents had established the association in 1954 to host birthday parties and holiday celebrations. They also funded upkeep for Belchertown's beloved and beautiful Stein and Goldstein carousel. In the late 1960s, the Friends campaigned publicly about problems at the school. My parents received its newsletters in the mail, and I skimmed through them from time to time.

"Can we help with a Friends project?" I asked Papa one day as we drove to visit Mary Jean.

"We live too far away," he said. "Besides, I don't agree with their politics."

"What politics?" I asked.

"How many times do I have to tell you to mind your own business?"

"Well, I know you don't like Ben Ricci," Mom said quietly.

"Shut up and let me drive."

Mom and I went back to reading our books.

I learned more about Ben Ricci in 2005 when I came across his book, *Crimes Against Humanity*, while researching the history of Belchertown State School. Like Mary Jean and the Parks' daughter, Jessy, Ben and Ginnie Ricci's son Bobby was evaluated at Boston Children's Hospital, and in 1952, at the age of five, he was diagnosed with mental retardation. Ricci was faced with the same difficult choice given to my parents.

In his book he wrote, "The spokesman for the [doctors] started off with a statement that caused my hopes to rise. 'It is our considered judgment,' said the senior physician, 'that you have a choice …' I took advantage of the slight pause in his delivery to ponder that statement. A choice. Not bad, I thought. At least we have a choice. What a precious opportunity. Then came the measured words, delivered without emotion by the doctor who obviously had delivered bad tidings before. 'You have a choice which involves your family.' The choice was between us — the family unit — or Bobby's continued presence with us. 'The stress upon a growing family that the presence of a hyperactive, retarded child exerts is often intolerable, and in most cases, causes undesirable psychological and emotional harm. Your choice is between a somewhat normal family life and a hectic future with likely detrimental effects upon all family members.' The doctors were of one opinion: they strongly recommended that Bobby be 'institutionalized.'"

The Riccis placed Bobby in Belchertown in 1953. Like Mom and Papa, they trusted the experts' recommendations. I don't know if doctors in Massachusetts during the 1950s and '60s were ignorant about conditions at Belchertown, or if they knew and believed that the suffering of these children mattered less than the stress or inconvenience to "normal" family members.

After a year of visits to Belchertown, hearings, and a review of documents and memos, the state legislature's Joint Commission concluded in its 1971 report that the school was "a product of monumental administrative neglect, inertia, and malpractice." Findings included the absence of basic sanitation and hygiene, intolerably inadequate medical care, frequent incidents of maltreatment, and cruel, abusive punishment. Raw sewage backed up and flowed onto floors. Excrement and urine were constantly visible. The report also criticized the way the state Department of Mental Health responded to the "The Tragedy of Belchertown" articles.

The newspaper series and the Joint Commission's report brought fighting among individuals and groups to a fevered pitch. Commissioner Dr. Milton Greenblatt fired Dr. Wakstein, the regional administrator who had cooperated with Shanks' investigation, for disloyalty. The school's trustees claimed "The Tragedy of Belchertown" articles were filled with falsehoods and half-truths. Belchertown State School employees called for the resignation of Superintendent Bowser. Bowser's supporters cited the improvements he'd made during his administration. A week after the Commission released its report, Bowser and most of the trustees resigned.

My father had little interest in the administrative clashes at Belchertown. Instead, he focused attention on additional funding for institutions available through the Medicaid program. In the final days of 1971, federal legislation expanded the definition of an intermediate care facility to include services for eligible individuals residing in qualified public mental retardation institutions. A significant proportion of the cost for Medicaid clients in these facilities would be covered if the state complied with detailed federal standards for facilities, programs, and services. He was sure that Belchertown's administrators, whoever they might be, would make the necessary changes to meet the new standards, even though he'd experienced first-hand the dreadful conditions.

However, families and professionals working to develop community-based options worried that directing more federal funds to institutions would be a disincentive for the Massachusetts legislature to support group homes. The conflict diminished somewhat after the creation of the federal Supplemental Security Income program in 1972, which provided benefits that could be used by eligible individuals with disabilities to cover the costs of community-based care. Yet the tension — and competition for dollars — between proponents of institutions and advocates for home-based care continues today.

When frustration with conditions at Belchertown drove Ben Ricci to consider suing the state bureaucracy, he was turned down by fifteen lawyers. He then approached Beryl Cohen, who had served as counsel to the Joint Commission that investigated Belchertown in 1970. Cohen suggested a class-action lawsuit, in which a small group files and prosecutes on behalf of a larger group. Wanting secrecy during the planning stage, Ricci invited about thirty-five relatives and friends of potential class members, including board members of the Friends Association, to his home in Amherst. To the best of my knowledge, my parents were not invited. After discussion about potential retribution by the state, the Friends Association board voted to hire Cohen and move ahead. Ricci and Cohen selected twenty-six people as co-plaintiffs.

In February 1972, the group filed a class action in federal court on behalf of more than 1,000 Belchertown residents, including Mary Jean, alleging the state was denying residents' constitutional right to adequate living conditions and treatment. Ricci's son, Robert Simpson Ricci, was the lead plaintiff. The Commissioner of the Massachusetts Department of Mental Health was the lead defendant. The fifty-two-page complaint listed appalling conditions and made claims for relief under both Massachusetts law and the United States Constitution.

The state Attorney General's office asserted residents didn't have a constitutional right to make demands because they were voluntarily admitted to Belchertown. The state denied almost every allegation in the suit, even those that the Department of Mental Retardation had acknowledged. Some Belchertown staff signed on as friends of the court in support of the *Ricci* plaintiffs.

At first, it seemed that the class action would proceed quickly. Four days after filing, Judge Francis W. Ford issued a preliminary restraining order. "I never knew such things existed as the issues that were raised in the complaint," he said.

The restraining order prohibited Belchertown administrators from admitting additional residents until they presented a plan for the orderly reduction of the population. They also were forbidden from transferring residents to state facilities for the mentally ill. Judge Ford directed the state Secretary for Human Services to evaluate all residents' medical needs within thirty days. Administrators were ordered to fill staff vacancies, make repairs, purchase supplies, and develop care-improvement plans.

But progress came to an abrupt stop when 90-year-old Judge Ford announced he would be lightening his caseload by giving up his civil cases. The *Ricci* case was reassigned to 72-year-old Judge Anthony Julian, who retired a few months later. His replacement, Judge Levin Campbell, allowed the plaintiffs' motion for class certification but soon after was appointed to the Court of Appeals. The next reassignment was to Judge Manual Real, a visiting judge from the U.S.

District Court in Los Angeles. The case was permanently reassigned to Judge Joseph L. Tauro of the U.S. District Court of Massachusetts fourteen months after Judge Ford issued the restraining order.

Change did not come quickly enough. Four Belchertown residents, all young adults, died at the end of 1971. Chris Adams choked on his dinner. John Abbot swallowed an open safety pin and punctured his carotid artery. Rena Aubin ate so much that her stomach ruptured. Linda Buchanan wandered away from her building and died of exposure on the school grounds. Linda's freedom to be outside had been an attempt to "normalize" the environment. However, the unlocked doors policy did not come with money for additional staff to appropriately supervise residents.

When Chris choked, an attendant and a doctor tried to revive him. The doctor was one of six foreign-educated physicians on the Belchertown staff who hadn't yet received a license to practice in Massachusetts outside the school.

Overcrowding, understaffing, and inadequate medical services contributed to these deaths. Many staff members were deeply shaken. Good people worked at Belchertown alongside indifferent ones. The fundamental problem was that the school lacked enough adequately trained and compensated staff to provide appropriate care.

During my senior year in high school, I walked to the Berkshire Athenaeum at least once a week looking for new articles about Belchertown.

After I told the reference librarian that I was doing a research project on Belchertown — not *exactly* true — she showed me how to use the index of periodicals to make sure I didn't miss relevant stories. The librarian was the only person who knew what I was reading. Papa would have slapped my face — or worse — if he had found out. He wanted the publicity to stop. I wanted it to continue.

The articles confirmed all the things I'd seen and heard and smelled for ten years. Sometimes, after reading about the atrocities so familiar to me, I dashed to the ladies' room to vomit. But I was relieved the world was waking up to the truth.

Joe Klein, then a young reporter for the Boston *Real Paper* alternative weekly, wrote an article about the four deaths, headlined "Belchertown: Budget Cuts Kill Kids." He went on to a distinguished career in journalism and wrote the best seller *Primary Colors*.

In an eerie echo of my father's stated wish that God would just take Mary Jean, Klein quoted a staff member: "…I must admit that almost all the parents whose children died seemed to breathe a sigh of relief. Of course, they feel tremendous guilt, but I think they're glad the children are finally out of their misery."

Another parent, whose child died of neglect, reflected the guilt and hopelessness of the situation: "Neither of us can do anything to move the bureaucracy. Even if I gave you my side of the story, it would just be my word against theirs. And they'd say I was just a hysterical mother. It's my fault anyway. I signed my child into that place. I had to say that my child was a menace to society . . . That's what you have to do to put someone in Belchertown. And all I can say is that between us, me and the state did a great job of murdering my child."

Klein wrote: "It is a nightmare of a system in which outrageous behavior is rewarded, but passivity is the ideal. It is a system of negative reinforcement: an attendant, faced with forty screaming patients to look after, is only able to respond to a crisis. The residents learn the way to get attention is to provoke a fuss, so there's competition of sorts to see who can behave the worst. The result is that within six months after being admitted, many of the retarded have deteriorated emotionally. For a long time . . . the only people interested in improving the institutions like Belchertown were the parents of the retarded, and they were so loaded with guilt about dumping their kids in the state schools, and so fearful that if they caused a ruckus their children would be thrown out, that they didn't push too hard. One mother, who found her child bruised and scarred every time she visited said, 'For a long time I was so ashamed. I was afraid to speak up. Now I'm just angry. If the government came into my house and found me treating my son the way he's been treated at Belchertown, I'd be arrested for child abuse.'"

Klein concluded, "Belchertown is a death factory, a hell-hole that continues to be tolerated, despite numerous reports of disgusting conditions and plans to make it fit for humans, dating back to 1964."

When I read the *Real Paper* article, I felt close to having a nervous breakdown. To deal with my rage, I channeled energy into my high school debate team. Maybe I couldn't lash out at home about the Belchertown atrocities — or the mayhem in my head and chest every time I was in the same room with Papa — but I could ferociously deliver arguments at competitions.

The debate resolution my senior year focused on the federal government providing a program of comprehensive medical care for all citizens. I spent hours at the library, documenting my research on three-by-five index cards and organizing them in a heavy grey metal carrying case that I locked to keep out the prying eyes of competitors. I practiced endlessly with Jimmy, my debate partner, switching between pro and con roles so the coin toss that determined which position we'd take wouldn't rattle our confidence.

I was a skilled debater, alert for the missteps of the other team and ready to pounce for the kill. Few girls debated during those years, and I was proud when I routinely walked away with the win, except for one incident.

The debate was typical, and my voice was vehement as I finished my closing statement. I looked up and saw one of the boys on the other team sobbing silently. He sniffled and wiped his nose with the sleeve of his white dress shirt. The judges averted their eyes as both teams left to wait in the cafeteria for the results.

"You won again," our coach, Mr. Conklin, said twenty minutes later as he approached Jimmy and me. "Good job."

"I quit," I said.

"Pardon me?" said Mr. Conklin.

"What the heck?" asked Jimmy.

"I quit. This is wrong. I can't do this anymore. It's not right to make someone cry."

Jimmy shot me a disgusted look.

"Why don't you sleep on it?" Mr. Conklin suggested.

When I didn't change my mind, Mr. Conklin asked me to stop by his classroom after school a few weeks later.

"Sharon, you've already qualified for the state tournament. There's an event that we don't have at Pittsfield High, but you might want to give it a try. It's called group discussion. Kids from different schools are put in a group. You get scored both on your arguments and on how well you help other kids get their points across."

As sure as I was about my decision to quit debating, I was disappointed that I wouldn't go to the state tournament. I was intrigued by this new opportunity and agreed to do it.

"Great," said Mr. Conklin. "Here's a pamphlet with the rules."

A few weeks later, kids from our school climbed onto a chartered bus with the debate teams from the other two high schools in Pittsfield. I got a headache on the drive down Route 7 to the turnpike but rallied and enjoyed the three group discussion rounds. I grabbed a Coke and a bag of Fritos from the snack area and waited in an auditorium for the award ceremony. I wasn't surprised when my name was not called.

As we lined up to get back on the bus, Mr. Conklin handed the judges' scoring sheet to each of us. I scanned my results. Of five categories, I received the full twenty points in four, and nineteen in the fifth area. Total: Eighty-one. What? My total should be ninety-nine! One point off from one hundred is ninety-nine. I ran to Mr. Conklin, who was standing with the other coaches.

"This is wrong, Mr. Conklin!" I shouted. "They added my score wrong!"

He took the sheet from me. "This is a problem," he said. "Wait here."

I got back on the bus and waited. The other kids were tired and impatient. I kept my head down, hoping that no one would notice the delay was my fault. We waited. And waited. Finally, Mr. Conklin got on the bus and approached me.

"Sharon, you won. You won the gold medal."

Tears of frustration and satisfaction filled my eyes. I did not know it at the time, but my ability to help others articulate their thoughts would become the focal point of my career as a consultant and facilitator.

"They won't take away the medals they awarded in the auditorium, but they'll mail a gold medal to you. The next highest score was 97."

The bus back to Pittsfield was almost an hour late. Most parents seemed anxious as they milled around in the parking lot. Papa had stayed in his VW bug, clearly annoyed.

"Why can't they give parents the right information?" he barked.

"Well, there was a problem," I said and explained the scoring mishap and our delayed departure.

"I don't know why you had to make a fuss," he snapped. "Why do you always have to be the best?"

12

SEEKING SOLACE

As I was counting the weeks until high school graduation, Judge Tauro decided to see firsthand whether grounds existed for the class-action complaints. He asked his law clerk and attorneys from both sides to join him at Belchertown. The judge later said that when they arrived at the main gate for a surprise inspection tour, he wondered if he'd overreacted. It was a beautiful day, and the campus was quite attractive with brick buildings and carefully manicured, rolling lawns. As he stepped from the car he thought, "This is a waste of time. What are we doing here? Then we went inside. The conditions were even worse than described in the complaint. There was constant noise and screaming, half-naked residents lying unattended on the floor. Flies and mosquitoes flew freely because there were no screens on the windows, which meant that bodies of the residents were covered with insect bites. There was clogged plumbing, unattended residents drinking out of the commodes, and an overwhelming stench of urine and feces. And there was just incessant screaming, almost like there was a soundtrack of horrible screaming. I spent nine hours touring every square

126

foot of Belchertown that day. It was the most punishing experience of my life."

Mary Jean lived in one of the buildings that Judge Tauro visited. At the conclusion of the tour, he convened a brief meeting in the parking lot. The case collapsed when the judge said it would not be possible for the Commonwealth to come up with any sort of expert opinion that would convince him that little girls are supposed to drink out of urinals, that there were supposed to be welts all over people's bodies, that there were supposed to be feces all over the floor, that people were supposed to be unclothed, writhing in obvious pain.

He directed the Assistant Attorney General to inform the Governor and Attorney General about his visit. There will be no trial, he said. Only a consent agreement. No possible expert testimony could convince him that the conditions he'd seen were the way it was supposed to be.

Judge Tauro explained that the law is very clear that if you take a view, and notice is given to everybody, then what the judge sees, or what the jury sees, is evidence, just as though you took photographs and marked them with exhibition stickers. He said, "To find the facts, all I would have to do was recite my memories, and there was no evidence available to contradict what we saw. Instead of wasting time litigating the impossible, why don't we go right to the remedial phase. Let's see if we can start the world all over again, and without pointing fingers of blame at anybody, just come up with a consensual, remedial program that will put this institution closer to the 21st century than the 19th century."

During the next five months, Judge Tauro held long and frequent negotiations in his chambers. He actively participated in the discussions, often reaching into his pocket for cash and sending someone out for coffee and donuts. The consent decree was signed on November 13, 1973.

Judge Tauro presided over the class action for more than two decades, forcing the state to spend millions on improving care. He held regular status conferences in his chambers with lawyers and visited Belchertown and four other state-run schools to check progress. When he became frustrated by the slow pace of the changes the consent decree demanded, he added U.S. Secretary of Health and Human Services Margaret Heckler as a party to the lawsuit, arguing that federal funds weren't being spent properly. When Heckler threatened to withhold millions of federal dollars, the Massachusetts legislature finally agreed to fund implementation of the consent decree. The *Ricci* case defined Judge Tauro's career and legacy: He was widely recognized and respected as a champion for people with disabilities.

My parents had been an emotional mess after the "Tragedy of Belchertown" articles were published, and things got worse as the *Ricci* class action unfolded. Papa would rant about the Friends of Belchertown or Judge Tauro, then retreat to his bedroom to find relief in saying the rosary and imploring the Virgin Mary to intercede and stop the publicity. Mom was less comforted by religion. She tried to pray, but she said the prayers felt empty.

They eventually found a kind of solace in the summer of 1972 when they joined a spiritual movement called the Catholic charismatic renewal, a blend of Catholic teachings and Pentecostal-style prophecy and faith healing. Adherents take literally John the Baptist's promise that the Messiah will baptize believers in the Holy Spirit and in fire. Mom and Papa attended frequent prayer groups at Sacred Heart Church, some for men, some for women, and some mixed gender. Although Mom and Papa continued to go to occasional weekday masses at Sacred Heart, for Sunday mass they switched to Cranwell, a Jesuit prep school in nearby Lenox where several of the priests were charismatic renewal leaders.

When Mom and Papa attended their first prayer meeting, I was seventeen and midway through my first stretch of time away from home. Aunt El had died a year earlier from a massive stroke and left my family a small inheritance that allowed me to attend a program in Bavaria the summer after my junior year. The freedom from Papa's control was wondrous. For the first time, I could make my own choices, speak freely, and have fun without the burden of his pervasive disapproval. I ate cream-filled pastries for breakfast. I hung out with American and German kids at pubs after our morning school sessions, drinking Weissbier and snacking on sausages. I went dancing in clubs and hiking in the Alps. I made more close friends during those six weeks than I had made at any school in Pittsfield. Good feelings — relief, enthusiasm, connection, hope — slowly pushed their way through the barricade I'd constructed against the pain of hating who I was.

Upon my return, Mom told me about the prayer group on the long drive home from JFK Airport in New York City. "It's the most amazing thing," she gushed. "You have to come with us! You'll love it!"

I wasn't interested. My heart was still in Germany, and I deeply missed my new friends. Before the trip, I had been excited about my senior year of high school, but I came home thinking school was lame. I expected to recover from jet lag in a few days, but my fatigue went on for weeks. Nothing was interesting or fun. Looking back, I realize that I was depressed.

Desperate for connections with other people, I finally decided to try a prayer meeting with Mom and Papa.

The power of community was strong and affected me deeply. I was welcomed with enthusiasm and attended prayer meetings at least once a week. In the early fall, my parents told me my high school graduation gift would be a plane ticket to South Bend, Indiana, to attend a rally at the University of Notre Dame. Sixty-thousand charismatic Catholics would be singing and praying in tongues in the football stadium. They felt sure that this trip would be life-changing, and the perfect way to move into adulthood.

Mom and Papa were set on my attending a Catholic college, where they believed professors would censor books and protect me from dangerous ways of thinking. But my high school biology teacher suggested I check out Williams College, in the small town about twenty miles from Pittsfield where Clara Claiborne Park lived and her husband was a professor. Clara's book about autism had continued to haunt me.

I drove alone to the interview on a spectacular autumn day because Papa had a migraine. When I arrived at the small white clapboard building that housed the admissions office, a secretary greeted me warmly. A student walked a small group of teenagers and their parents around campus for a tour. While I was embarrassed to be the only one there without family, I also felt relieved I didn't have to worry about my parents' reactions. I could imagine living in the freshman quad and attending classes in small seminar rooms. My interview with the director of admissions was a long, animated conversation. As we wrapped up, he asked if I'd considered applying for early decision.

"What's that?" I asked. He'd put me so at ease that I overcame my usual reluctance to admit that I didn't know something.

"That means that you apply right away and, if we accept you in December, you agree to come here without applying to other colleges."

I returned home determined to apply early decision to Williams. Papa argued against it, saying that ideas could infect my mind and put my eternal soul at risk.

"Once you get an idea in your head, you can never get it out," he insisted.

"That's ridiculous," I told him. "I'm perfectly capable of figuring out what I believe. If an idea doesn't make sense, I'll toss it. My brain will be just fine, I'm sure."

Mom didn't say much at the time, but she later told me that she and Papa only agreed to let me apply because they were sure I would not be accepted. The historically all-male college had gone co-ed just two years earlier. To placate alumni worried about how fewer men might affect athletic programs, the college decided to slowly increase the school's size. This meant intense competition for the limited spots available to women.

My acceptance letter arrived just before Christmas. Despite their concerns, Mom and Papa allowed me to go to Williams in the fall. And as they had feared, my commitment to the charismatic renewal did not survive my freshman year of college. I became increasingly disillusioned with the beliefs my parents found so sustaining. When I attended prayer meetings during college breaks, I watched the men assert dominance over their wives and children, citing biblical passages about women being silent and submitting to their husbands. I was dismayed by self-serving prophecies that purportedly came from the Holy Spirit. I was troubled by the feverish control the prayer group leaders held over the rank-and-file. The intense chauvinism in the group mirrored the deep patriarchy I was coming to recognize in the Catholic church as a whole and in my family.

I realized that the truly dangerous ideas in my head were not coming from ideas in books, but from the traditional Catholic doctrines I'd learned as a child and the cult-like beliefs of the charismatic renewal. When I thought about it, the Baltimore catechism that the nuns made me memorize in elementary school didn't make sense. Our parish priest's admonition about the menace of my body as a vessel of sin, delivered from behind the confessional booth's screen when I was thirteen, was demeaning. The lesson from another priest during an after-school religion class that my parents forced me to attend in high school was laughable: It was not a sin to kiss, he claimed, it was only a sin to enjoy it. The church's insistence that only men could be ordained to the priesthood devalued and disempowered women. The ideas I'd learned through the church, I realized, posed a grave danger to the likelihood I'd live a full and satisfying life.

Like a skin that no longer fit, I began a years-long process of casting off the charismatic renewal and the church as a whole. I took a few tentative steps away from the church when I married Peter Hyde in June 1975, the end of my sophomore year of college and the weekend of his graduation. We'd met through the Newman Association, an organization for Catholic students, and we often talked about our dismay at the church's tenets and practices. To please my parents, we agreed that three Catholic priests, friends of theirs from the charismatic renewal, would officiate at our wedding in the College chapel. During a pre-nuptial meeting, one of the priests granted our request to write our vows and the prayers for the mass. But contrary to the agreed-upon plan, the priests also went through the entire traditional ceremony. It was unbearably long. I was angry that the priests ignored our wishes. And although I was grateful for the family and friends who shared in our celebration, I felt a deep sadness that Mary Jean was not with us.

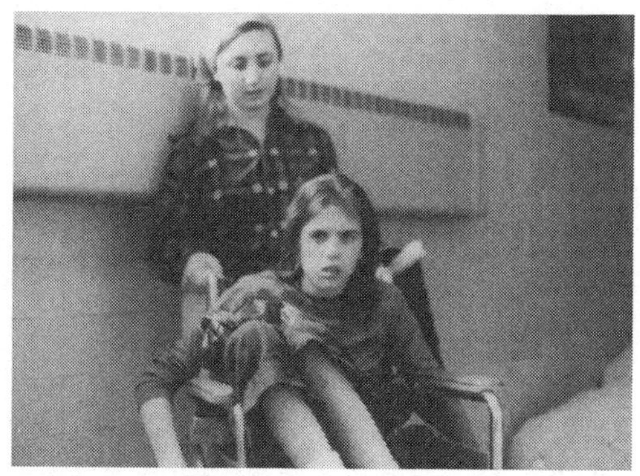

*Sharon and Mary Jean —
Belchertown State School, 1975*

Mary Jean — Belchertown State School, 1975

My parents remained fervent Catholics and charismatics throughout their lives, although they experienced different degrees of faith. Papa's devotion to the Virgin Mary and his belief that she interceded on his behalf never wavered. He was confident his sins were forgiven. Mom had doubts. Guilt about sending Mary Jean to Belchertown wracked her days and nights. As she approached the end of life, she was scared that heaven did not await. The church and the charismatic renewal were not enough to console her.

13

LEAVING BELCHERTOWN

Mom called me one day in 1976. "Tim got involved with the trouble at Belchertown," she said casually. "There's some sort of labor dispute and he's worried about Mary Jean, but I'm sure it's nothing."

It was something. For three days, about 20,000 state workers in western Massachusetts went on strike to demand a living wage. Even though a judge declared the strike illegal, workers blocked the entrance to Belchertown State School and other facilities in the state with picket lines. When he heard about the strike, Tim drove from his college apartment in southern New Hampshire to check on Mary Jean. Dozens of strikers swarmed the school's driveway. An article in *The Springfield Morning Union* recounted the scene: "'Scabs! Strikebreakers! Go on working, you bunch of suckers, instead of fighting for our cause!' came the jeers of the strikers, several dozen strong. They greeted every car that way. . . . One employee carried a sign reading: 'Slavery died 100 years ago, or didn't you know?'"

Screaming obscenities, strikers threw rocks and pounded on the hood of Tim's car as he tried to drive through the commotion. He was afraid he'd be killed. He backed up a bit and then accelerated forward, playing a game of chicken with the most aggressive strikers. At the last moment, they jumped aside. Faced with a second picket line, Tim abandoned his car. As he made his way toward Mary Jean's building, a man threatened him with a steel pole. Tim knocked the pole to the ground and stepped on it; the man backed down and Tim pushed on.

It took him a long time to find Mary Jean. Staff had tied down residents before leaving them unattended, with neither food nor sanitation. He released Mary Jean from her restraints and heated canned food in the kitchen for as many residents as he could manage. "A few workers came in for the night shift after the media and cameras were gone," he later said. "It was hard to leave Mary Jean there, but at least there were some attendants."

His leave-taking was not easy — a Massachusetts state trooper stood next to his car. Why had he tried to run people down? Tim told his story and got off with a warning. He left Belchertown emotionally bruised and shaken.

However, his telephone calls to my parents and newspaper articles about the strike didn't cause Mom and Papa to drive to Belchertown and check on Mary Jean. On the contrary, they decided to postpone a planned visit until after the trouble died down. Tim's willingness to put his life on hold to step up and protect Mary Jean would be repeated many times in the years ahead. In contrast, my parents retreated behind a barricade of denial, continuing to tell themselves that even with the staggering problems, Mary Jean was better off at Belchertown.

Shortly after Mary Jean turned eighteen in 1977, Mom and Papa filed a "Guardianship of Mentally Retarded" petition to ensure that they would remain Mary Jean's legal guardians. As much as they didn't want responsibility for her day-to-day care, they didn't want to cede decision-making control to the state.

Later that year, Mary Jean had surgery for an aneurysm in the axillary artery of her right arm. In a delicate operation, a surgeon placed a permanent shunt under her arm. The Belchertown doctor who explained the situation said it was probably a congenital defect, but my parents suspected it was caused by an injury, perhaps from someone hitting her. The cause of such an aneurysm is almost always severe blunt force trauma. Despite the class-action consent decree, Mary Jean was still not safe.

Although my parents had opposed the suit, Mary Jean was one of the more than 1,000 members of the *Ricci* class. The consent decree required Belchertown State School to implement changes in the physical environment and rehabilitative services and develop a community-based service system. Mom and Papa's longtime fear that Mary Jean would be moved back to her home community was becoming reality. She would no longer be segregated in an institution far from home.

The consent decree called for placement in a residential environment close to her family and in the least restrictive and most normal setting appropriate to her needs. The setting was to be integrated with the "non-retarded community" to the fullest extent possible. Her living environment must be safe, humane, clean, healthy, and appropriate. Along with other environmental conditions, the decree dictated the placement must be designed to provide maximum habilitation, privacy, accessibility, and training. Services had to comply with federal and state constitutional requirements. The federal court empowered a court monitor to supervise the defendants' obligations to the class members.

In theory, the terms of the consent decree would forever protect Mary Jean from horrors like those she experienced at

Belchertown. She had a long list of entitlements. She would have an annual, written Individual Service Plan, known as an ISP, which specified in detail her capabilities and service needs. The ISPs would document the methods used to provide services throughout her life. Her guardian would approve the methods. She would have active treatment and a habilitation program with care, training, and education to help her lead a life as close to normal as possible.

The consent decree spelled out class members' rights regarding personal dignity, freedom from physical or psychological abuse and mistreatment, restraints, and inappropriate medication. Mary Jean was guaranteed medical, recreational, educational, and transportation services. Her meals would be appropriate, sufficient, and well-balanced, and she'd have adequate clothing, linen, and laundry. Respite care services, temporary residential assistance, and emergency crisis intervention services were to be readily available.

As a member of the *Ricci* class, Mary Jean was guaranteed funding for a level of care and services that was unprecedented in Massachusetts. It sounded great, but no one was sure how it would play out.

In May 1978, at age nineteen, Mary Jean was discharged from Belchertown State School. My parents' dread that they would have to bring her to their home didn't materialize. The state arranged for Mary Jean to be transported to West House, a group home in Pittsfield operated by the Berkshire County Association for Retarded Citizens, the agency responsible for her care. She attended day habilitation sessions — day-hab — through the Pittsfield public school system on weekdays. Mom and Papa said she was doing well, but I was skeptical. For all of Mary Jean's life, they had claimed she was healthier and happier than was ever true.

Peter and I moved to Ohio in 1977. We visited Mary Jean in the group home on trips back to Berkshire County. It was clean and nicely furnished, but Mary Jean continued to bite her wrists and bang her head against walls. She appeared to understand things people said to her but spoke only a few words. Instead of language, she used things she could control to communicate what she wanted, what she did not want, and when she was in pain. She often snapped her neck and screamed. She made loud noises and bit other people's arms. She hit and kicked workers and pulled their hair. She stuck her fingers down her throat to induce vomiting. She was capable of using the bathroom properly, but she urinated and defecated in places other than a toilet. She took off her clothes in public.

Most of the time, the people caring for her failed to interpret the underlying meaning of her behavior and respond appropriately. It wasn't until she fainted during a fire drill at her day-hab program, for example, that a doctor at the hospital diagnosed a serious urinary tract infection. No one had noticed her pain or fever.

Mary Jean lived in several different group homes during the 1980s and 1990s, all staffed by low-paid, under-trained workers. Employee turnover was high. Mary Jean's behavioral and mental health issues continued. She often experienced physical pain that led to tantrums. Premenstrual syndrome caused significant discomfort each month, and she had frequent foot pain. Changes such as new staff members and houses increased her distress. She slept too much during the day and not enough at night. Loud noises upset her. She ate very rapidly at meals, probably a holdover from having to fight for food at Belchertown. Her limited ability to communicate fear, frustration, discomfort, pain, and anger left her literally bruised and scarred.

Yet there were positives in Mary Jean's life. She developed affectionate relationships with some staff and other residents in the group homes. She liked to choose her own clothes and could name colors and shapes. She enjoyed music. When she wasn't in pain, she sang and danced.

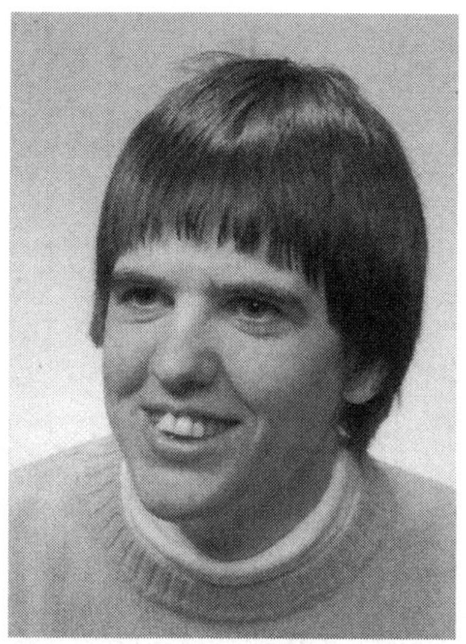

Mary Jean — Pittsfield, early 1980s

Belchertown was still open, but the population was dwindling, and there was never any talk of Mary Jean returning. The institution was still notorious. A 1985 article in *The Berkshire Eagle* recalled the scandal in 1971 when Belchertown was recognized as "... a dumping ground for retarded people, a filthy, fetid zoo of forgotten souls. Dark as that period was, it has had a positive repercussion. Out of it came Chapter 766, a state reform that demands retarded citizens be recognized as human . . ."

Eileen, Paul, and I left Pittsfield when we were young adults. Although we weren't in day-to-day contact with Mary Jean, she inspired our careers. For many years, Paul served as a shared living provider and held jobs supporting people with developmental disabilities. He frequently offered suggestions about services for Mary Jean. Eileen, while working on a master's in elementary education, was a one-on-one classroom aide for a young girl with autism whose mannerisms and behavior were uncannily similar to Mary Jean's. As a consultant to nonprofits and government agencies, I've guided collaborations that led to systems-level improvements for people with a range of disabilities.

Tim, a college professor in Pittsfield, became the sibling most involved with Mary Jean's care. As Mom and Papa aged and faced a growing list of health problems, Tim stepped in, although my parents remained her legal guardian throughout their lives. His success as a fierce advocate for Mary Jean — and the larger community of people with developmental disabilities — was affirmed when he received a letter from the governor commending his efforts.

Mom, Mary Jean, and Papa — Pittsfield, 1980s

Mom and Mary Jean —
House on Concord Parkway, Pittsfield, 1980s

Mary Jean —
Cottage on Pontoosuc Lake, Pittsfield, 1980s

My parents' intense emotional distress during their later years extended beyond their worry and guilt about Mary Jean. During the thirty-three years that Papa worked at General Electric, he was exposed daily to dangerous chemicals, including polychlorinated biphenyls, a group of synthetic compounds known as PCBs. The chemicals often spilled on his work clothes, which he threw in the bathroom hamper. Mom washed his oil-laden overalls with the rest of the family laundry. Serious impacts on human health and the environment led many countries to ban or severely restrict PCBs during the 1970s. Both of my parents developed cancer, although it's impossible to know whether PCB exposure played a role.

In the late 1970s, Papa began complaining of head and facial pain triggered by movement and odors. In addition to the impact of exposure to dangerous chemicals, he also was under significant work stress. He was in his fifties. Although his bosses praised his execution of various projects, throughout his career he was told in performance reviews to improve the breadth and depth of his technical knowledge in math, chemistry, and physics. Supervisors said he lacked the technical sophistication in computer technology and analytical instrumentation that his job required. He took some courses to fill in gaps, but he was unable to reach the level of mastery expected of him. He struggled to maintain pride as he stepped back from his career and rued his decision, more than three decades earlier, to choose GE over the job at the dairy farm.

After a year on sick leave, he opted for early retirement at age sixty, which significantly decreased his retirement income. He and Mom fretted over money. He was restless after he stopped working. Gramp had moved in with them after Nana died in 1978, which Papa resented even though Mom did most of the work of caring for him. She endured Papa's daily diatribes about the inconvenience of having an old man suffering the after-effects of a stroke living in the den. Papa wanted to sell their Pittsfield house and move to Florida. He envisioned spending summers at the family cottage on Pontoosuc Lake in Pittsfield and the rest of the year in a warmer climate.

Mom disliked winter weather but couldn't imagine losing her home and leaving her father behind. By this time, she had achieved her dream of a colonial-style house on a parkway, the neighborhood that Nana had envisioned when we moved to Peck's Road so many years earlier. But after months of arguments, Papa prevailed. They moved Gramp to an assisted-living home in Pittsfield, and Mom and Papa relocated to Fort Myers, Florida. Mom grieved over leaving Gramp behind, but my parents had no concern about being so far away from Mary Jean. The agency would take care of her, they said, and she was too retarded to know they'd moved away.

They bought a pretty house in Florida with a screen-enclosed swimming pool and joined a prayer group and a bromeliad club to make friends. Papa enjoyed himself when he wasn't having pain or dizziness, but Mom worried about how her new acquaintances were judging the appropriateness of her prayers, her bromeliads, and her lemon bars. She began having panic attacks while driving. Soon the fear of a pounding heart and feeling faint kept her housebound unless Papa felt up to driving.

Mary Jean's health also continued to deteriorate. She was admitted to the psychiatric unit of Berkshire Medical Center in May 1989 for sustained out-of-control behavior. The psychiatrist said her problems escalated as a result of numerous environmental changes. Progress notes that year said Mary Jean "can be manipulative with staff" and expressed concern that her medications masked her capabilities and strengths. The conclusion was that Mary Jean "doesn't do well in a large residence and needs a supervised twenty-four-hour residential program with no more than three compatible peers."

The comment about manipulating staff alludes to an incident that reveals a great deal about Mary Jean's personality and capabilities. The protocol at the group home was to keep residents' medications in small paper bags labeled with their names and stored in an unlocked kitchen cabinet. Mary Jean intensely disliked the staff member who distributed the medications. Without being seen, Mary Jean removed a bag from the shelf, defecated in it, then put the bag back in place. When the worker put his hand into the bag, he grabbed a handful of shit.

Smart? Absolutely. The platitudes of doctors about children with severe mental retardation being blissfully unaware of their circumstances were blatantly untrue. Mary Jean liked some people and detested others. Her records show that she surprised staff with her ability to identify pictures when asked to point to objects and to survival signs — danger, poison, bus stop, stairs, fire exit, escalator, and others. She enjoyed sorting and matching games. She had a strong memory, learned new tasks quickly, and retained information easily. She readily learned signs in American Sign Language, but few staff could sign with her. She had strong preferences about the clothes she wore.

Her dislikes were intense, too. Chaotic situations and loud noises caused her to act out. She didn't want to wear shoes, probably because her feet hurt. She showed distress when she was ignored. Despite these behaviors, her program specialist described Mary Jean in 1990 as "a delightful woman with a wonderful personality." The specialist said that Mary Jean responded best to a low-key, unassuming approach. She was most calm when she was near a staff person.

Mary Jean was on half a dozen powerful psychotropic medications that had side effects. Doctors tried various combinations of drugs, but nothing moved her toward stability. After more than a decade in group homes, it was obvious to family and social workers that Mary Jean was not receiving the level of service she was entitled to under the *Ricci* consent decree. She could not be at peace or thrive in a large, noisy facility.

Tim confronted the area director of the state Department of Mental Retardation during a meeting.

"It was clear that Mary Jean needed one-to-one staffing, 24/7," Tim told me. "We were trying to figure out how that would work. Basically, we were inventing a shared-living model. However, the director made a veiled threat, telling me that if I continued to cause problems, Mary Jean might not get the care she needed."

Unlike many family members who are intimidated by the fear of retaliation, Tim picked up the phone hanging on the wall and dialed the extension for the director's secretary. He told her he was being threatened and asked her to send state troopers.

"I also asked her to put a call through to the governor's office because I wanted to speak to him," Tim recalled. "The director came over and took the phone. 'That won't be necessary,' he told his secretary. And with that, a more civil conversation began about Mary Jean's care."

As negotiations were underway, Mary Jean's health deteriorated. Brushing teeth had never been a Belchertown routine, and Mary Jean had developed severe periodontal disease. In August 1991, she had fifteen teeth extracted under general anesthesia. She weighed less than 100 pounds.

That same year, a psychiatrist said Mary Jean had mixed bipolar disorder. He observed that she quickly shifted between states of hypomania — a less extreme form of mania — and depression. He adjusted her medications during the hospitalization and again in the middle of January 1992. A week later, Mary Jean was admitted in a full-blown manic state to the Human Resource Institute, a psychiatric hospital in the Boston area. She also had pneumonia.

Her self-abuse had escalated to pulling out clumps of her hair, beating herself up, and biting. She pulled people's hair and kicked them. She paced in her hospital room and took off her clothes many times. Staff said she appeared to be quite frightened. The attending physician thought Mary Jean might be having a negative reaction to a drug added to her medication cocktail the week before, or that her deterioration might be in response to staff changes at her residential facility.

The doctor's notes said that Tim visited twice, as did staff from Mary Jean's residence. The doctor described Tim as invested in her well-being, supportive, and helpful. Mary Jean didn't respond to Tim's presence, probably because she was on multiple medications to calm her down. One-to-one sessions with hospital staff also had a calming effect. She was allowed to return to her room every time she appeared to be overstimulated in community areas. She left the facility with prescriptions for six different psychotropic drugs.

During this time, psychiatrists and developmental pediatricians in community practice were becoming aware that autism and severe intellectual disabilities sometimes co-exist. Mary Jean's records show that doctors considered the possibility that she had autism, but the diagnosis was ruled out in 1990. The intensity of her psychiatric symptoms and sparse historical records may have been barriers to a comprehensive evaluation.

As the year ended, the last Belchertown residents moved to their home communities and the institution was permanently shuttered and abandoned. State and town officials held closing ceremonies in front of the administration building on the last day of 1992.

The decade after Mary Jean left Belchertown was also turbulent for me. I was the mother of two young children, working part-time, trying to focus on creating a healthy home and making our community a safer place. I volunteered for a domestic violence shelter and led abuse prevention programs in elementary schools. I became a midwife's assistant, doula, and childbirth educator. I tried to act like I was doing all right, but the aftershocks of growing up in a household of constant fear and ongoing trauma were taking their toll. I was often engulfed by anger and rage. I came to recognize that Papa had isolated our family from neighbors and potential friends as ferociously as communities in earlier decades segregated people with disabilities.

Peter was a high school math and statistics teacher at several east coast boarding schools during the 1980s. We lived in dorm apartments, which allowed Peter to come home and change a diaper or play a bit when he had a free period between classes. But as our kids reached school age, it became increasingly difficult to balance dorm duty with bedtime baths and stories. We wanted a change — a big change. In 1989, we moved to Phoenix, Arizona.

Distance from my parents and siblings gave me the emotional space to begin confronting the fiends that prowled around me. My parents visited once and decided they hated the desert; they were quite content living near my sister Eileen, first in Florida and then in South Carolina. I loved the expansive landscape of the southwest. Paradoxically, I felt safest in wide open spaces. A therapist helped me make sense of the emotional and physical trauma I'd experienced as a child. I found ways to manage anxiety, depression, and post-traumatic stress disorder. Slowly, I began what will be a lifelong process of healing.

In 1993, my parents and Tim co-signed a letter to the state Department of Mental Retardation asking that

Mary Jean immediately be moved to a two-person staffed supported residence. The residential downsizing had been a recommendation in the Individual Service Plan for six years, and they noted that the agency had a contractual responsibility to implement ISP recommendations in a timely manner.

Tim's insistence that Mary Jean be cared for in a shared-living model, where a client lives in a caretaker's private residence and receives 24/7 support, finally became a reality in 1994. The Department of Mental Retardation put out an "individual request for proposal" for a shared-living placement and awarded a contract to a local agency. Mary Jean moved in with a woman I'll call Laura, who had worked with Mary Jean in a group home, and her husband. The placement worked for a while. Social workers talked about "a new Mary Jean" who was happier, more stable, and much more communicative. They described her home environment as peaceful and stable. However, her day-hab program continued to be a source of stress. She was in a classroom with fourteen other people with significant needs and only two or three staff. She injured herself and wound up in the emergency room for stitches.

A social worker noted that the difference between her behavior at home and at day-hab was dramatic and warranted "a revisioning of Mary Jean on the part of many of her team members." The previous picture of Mary Jean was a woman with an organic brain disorder that caused severe acting-out behaviors. According to this analysis, psychotropic medications were needed to keep Mary Jean under control. But she was relatively calm and content at home, mostly acting out at day-hab. This suggested Mary Jean was a person with clear and well-defined preferences about her environment. If her services could be adapted to meet her preferences, she'd be less likely "to engage in maladaptive behaviors, and much more likely to have rewarding learning and personal growth experiences."

The social worker observed that Mary Jean could not process information successfully in a noisy or chaotic environment. Without one-on-one staff attention, she escalated negative behaviors to get attention. It was important to introduce unfamiliar staff gradually, with a familiar staff member present. All this was spelled out in a proposal for a new day program.

The proposal was never implemented.

Mary Jean's self-destructive behaviors, including self-induced vomiting, escalated until they were happening both at home and at the day-hab program. Two years after Mary Jean began living with Laura and her husband, they resigned as her caretakers when they couldn't get a second mortgage to expand their house.

Mary Jean's next several shared-living placements were unsuccessful. A shared-living approach can work if the caretaker is competent and compassionate, but for some people it's just a way to bring in significant cash, in much the same way as unethical providers take advantage of the foster care system. None of the new settings provided the quiet environment and consistent routine that Mary Jean needed. She expressed her anger by screaming, scratching, and hitting, disrobing and urinating or defecating in inappropriate places.

In 1996, Mary Jean was hospitalized again in the psychiatric unit at Berkshire Medical Center in Pittsfield, then transferred to Jewish Memorial Hospital and Rehabilitation Center near Boston. A neurologist noted that Mary Jean recently had an ear infection and a change in her living situation. It was clear Mary Jean's behavior deteriorated when she was in pain or had to contend with a change in routine.

During her inpatient stay, Mary Jean frequently banged her head hard against the wall, bit her arms, and stamped her feet. Staff tried to put her in a helmet and mittens, but she quickly found a way to take them off. When she became very agitated, staff put her in four-point restraints until a sedative took effect. A psychiatrist started her on yet another mixture of psychotropic drugs.

Mary Jean continued her desperate attempts to communicate through behavior, trying to let people know when she was in pain or didn't want to do something by making loud noises, hurting herself, or hurting others. Negative behaviors ranged from once or twice a week to ten times a day. An evaluating psychiatrist wrote that although she was frail and small, "her screaming is extremely loud and disruptive, and sounds like the soundtrack from a B-grade horror movie."

Caregivers and the psychiatrist described Mary Jean as pleasant and affectionate between crises. She was generally happy and easy to engage. She enjoyed being with caregivers, doing household activities and chores, going for rides in the car, and listening to music. She spoke a few words to make her desires known: "car ride" when she wanted to go for a short drive and "home" when she was tired. Rhythmic movement in a rocking chair helped her relax when she was upset. However, caregivers rarely managed to interpret her needs well enough to head off crises.

The chaos in Mary Jean's life mirrored quarrels between consumer advocates and state officials in Massachusetts during that time. The March 1996 issue of the *Advocacy Network News* claimed: "The Department of Mental Retardation is out of control. The agency is in a dizzying fall because of haphazard strategies and notable character flaws of its leadership. Tyrannical practices of coercion, intimidation, and suppression of information are practices throughout the system by too many of the DMR management. Morale is plummeting. Programs have gone haywire. Money is frittered away to support the personal ambitions of the DMR inner circle, their allies, and paid cronies."

In 1998, my brother Paul wrote a letter to the Massachusetts Department of Mental Retardation on Mary Jean's behalf. He listed a series of problems on the part of the agency responsible for her care and said the department was "a victim of a complete systems failure."

In late summer that year, the Department issued a request for what was termed a "consumer-directed request for responses" to "make more formal and lasting arrangements for Mary Jean." The Department invited my parents, Tim, and Paul to participate in interviews with six agencies. The agency that received the contract found a family that would take Mary Jean. The arrangement was marginally adequate, but ended three years later after her caregivers were abruptly forced to leave a rental home and couldn't find housing. Mary Jean ended up spending a weekend with a respite worker, who reported an increase in Mary Jean's self-abusive behaviors and anxiety.

The next placement in a shared-living home ended disastrously. A respite worker reported seeing the shared-living caretaker, Manzell Morton, smash a plate of food in Mary Jean's face and bend her feet back to her buttocks as she lay on the floor. The agency immediately removed Mary Jean from the home. Assault and battery charges were filed against Manzell.

A letter written by Manzell to the Commissioner of the Department of Mental Retardation, while not diminishing the abhorrence of her behavior, shines a spotlight on the lack of training for shared-living caretakers and the absence of adequate support at a system level.

Manzell was recovering from cancer. Three grandchildren, ages six, seven, and eighteen months, lived with her. She said the agency told her that Mary Jean pulled hair, bit herself, and screamed, but that she was not informed about other negative behaviors that occurred in past placements. Manzell claimed she was promised respite care, but respite workers weren't available or didn't show as scheduled.

She wrote, "Mary Jean pulled a lady's hair in the market and pulled my grandchildren's hair. She banged doors, kicked walls, and threw plates of food. She flipped my kitchen chairs and broke two. On one occasion she hit my granddaughter in the head. Breaking toilets was a past behavior in her last placement as well as here. I have holes in my walls in the room that was hers. I found out there were two families being considered for the client. The first one had been refused because of small children. Then how did I get her because I had small children also?"

Manzell admitted taking the disposable plate and pushing it in Mary Jane's face after a long morning of chaos and frustration. She denied bending Mary Jean's legs. And she decried the lack of careful consideration in making the placement, and the lack of resources and support she received: "I feel that my house was not the place for her because of the children, her behaviors, and all the problems with workers. . . . There was no plan, a lack of information, and poor assessment for proper placement played a factor, which led to this point. My training through the agency consisted only of a tape on fire safety. While I am not excusing my behavior that day, I feel that I was used. My grandchildren were placed in harm's way. I did not get the physical and mental support I was first promised. Untrained respite and day workers were placed in the position of learning to manage the client without proper clinical support. There are major factors that led to this incident."

In a letter to the court on behalf of Mary Jean, my brother Tim wrote that Mary Jean had been humiliated, degraded, and made to suffer when the person most responsible for her welfare failed to maintain self-control. He noted that Mary Jean lives with a medical condition — the shunt from her axillary artery aneurysm — that puts her at risk of hemorrhage when she is subjected to physical strain. This was documented in her Department of Mental Retardation records.

"In this context," Tim wrote in his statement, "one has to see that physical abuse of this profoundly incapacitated individual was not only outrageously wrong and immoral, it was also life-threatening assault and battery."

The senior investigator for the Massachusetts Disabled Persons Protection Commission determined that the allegations of physical and emotional abuse were substantiated. Manzell Morton was fired and charged with assault and battery of a retarded person. She pled guilty. The assistant district attorney told a reporter for *The Berkshire Eagle* that he was originally going to recommend jail time but changed his mind after meeting with the victim's brother.

Tim's reasons for opposing incarceration were complex and mirror the dilemmas still faced by the families of vulnerable people. The state Department of Mental Retardation and the provider agency were not about to assume blame for their failure to adequately train, supervise, and support a direct-service worker. It was in their interest to frame this as the bad actions of one individual.

But Mary Jean still needed care, and she already had a reputation in the developmental disability community as a challenging client. News that a caregiver ended up in jail might put Mary Jean on a whispered blacklist. Would she be deprived of a place to live and needed services? And Tim worried that the whole situation would be a setback for the shared-living model. Families often face hard choices: Will reporting abuse lead to retaliation? Will services be withheld from their loved ones? Tim made sure that Manzell would be prohibited from working as a caregiver but decided that Mary Jean's interests would not be served by Manzell going to jail.

After the assault in mid-May 2002, Mary Jean spent two nights with a respite worker and was then placed in an emergency respite home in a small city in northern Berkshire County. Her social worker said Mary Jean was out of control. On May 19, while Mary Jean was away from the house with the respite worker, the emergency provider informed the agency that they did not want her to return. Mary Jean spent the night at the respite worker's home and then stayed at the family cottage on Pontoosuc Lake over Memorial Day weekend, supported by the respite worker and other staff. The situation was desperate.

On May 28, Mary Jean was transported to Arbour-Fuller Hospital, a psychiatric facility in South Attleboro, Massachusetts. During her stay, she threw herself on the ground and sustained an injury that required an x-ray to check for a fracture. Doctors adjusted her medications in an attempt to control behaviors with less sedation. As the end of June approached, Arbour-Fuller doctors said she was ready for discharge.

Case workers at the agency responsible for Mary Jean's care were at a loss. They'd seen failure after failure in group homes and shared-living situations. They knew that Mary Jean's most immediate need was consistent attention and a quiet environment. They set up a meeting with shared-living providers Julie and David Morgan, who they hoped would take Mary Jean into their home on an emergency basis. If they said no, the case workers were out of options.

14
COMING HOME

"No one told us about the dying, the sickness, and the tragedy when we began shared-living two years prior, but that is another story of a different nature," Julie Morgan told me when I asked why she and her husband, David, accepted Mary Jean as a client in 2002. "This is a story of joy, success, and of coming home."

Julie began by telling me about their first two clients, both former residents of Belchertown State School. One lived with them for year before a childhood injury took his life. Next was Charlie, who had entered Belchertown as a newborn. He had Down syndrome and an atrial septal defect. After a year with Julie and David, Charlie had open-heart surgery and died after three months in the coronary care unit.

When they were considering taking on Mary Jean, David asked the social workers — I'll call them Tina and Joe — if Mary Jean, 42 years old at the time, was a screamer. Joe replied, "All the time."

"Is she self-abusive?" David continued.

"Constantly," Joe said.

David looked worried. "How is she on stairs?"

Joe said, "She throws herself down them."

Julie remembers feeling grim, but she asked, "Is she affectionate?"

Tina answered with a thoughtful "Yes." Joe nodded his agreement.

Julie asked, "Does she have a sense of humor?"

"Yes!" came without hesitation.

Julie decided that if Mary Jean could love and be loved, and laugh, there was a chance it would work out. Joe and Tina visited the couple's house to see if there would be a suitable room. They liked the soundproofed room designed by previous owners for their drum-playing son. It was perfect for a woman who screamed all the time, or rather, during the few hours that her medications allowed her to be awake.

"Mary Jean arrived on Friday, with piercing, wild green eyes and ready for action," Julie remembered. "My first response was to hug her. I told her that she was home now and would be safe. As she settled in, we were horrified to see the scars on her scalp, too many to count. She had a hole, gnawed to the bone, on her left arm. We were told it had been an open wound for three years. She was bald from pulling her hair out."

At first, Mary Jean seemed to feel safe and comfortable in her room but did not venture out very often. Gradually, she began spending time with the family in the kitchen and sunroom. The social workers wrote that during her first three weeks with the Morgans, they saw "a calmness that is unprecedented in the time we have served Mary Jean." They were pessimistic though, worried that old behaviors would return.

Julie and David tracked incidents of self-abuse and disruptive behaviors. Mary Jean had been given a new drug cocktail that seemed to be controlling violent outbursts, but she was sleeping eighteen hours a day. Difficult incidents were associated with specific places, people, and times. Eventually, negative behaviors went down from two a day to two a week to two a month.

Mary Jean soon was giving hugs and "Eskimo kisses," rubbing nose to nose, freely and often. "Folks were amazed that our daughter Lauren could get in her face without stressing her," Julie said. "She ate up the love."

"We waited for the other shoe to drop," Julie said. But it never did. Mary Jean had been with the Morgans for more than a decade when Julie told me this story. "The problem behaviors seemed to disappear. Completely. We call her 'Mary Dream.'"

Mary Jean was secure and truly at home in the Morgans' rambling house, built in 1801 on the bank of the east branch of the Housatonic River in Dalton, a small town adjacent to Pittsfield. During the warm months, geese feed on the broad lawn between the house and the river. Alcoves and additions have been added over the years, accommodating the changing needs and fortunes of its inhabitants. It's only feet away from Main Street, a road that was once a muddy path for horses and stagecoaches. The oldest part of the house served for years as the town's tiny post office.

By paying attention to her preferences, Julie transitioned Mary Jean's wardrobe from jeans with bibs to pretty blouses and dress pants. It turned out that Mary Jean liked to wear make-up and cologne. Her sense of humor started to emerge. "Knowing that I struggle with left and right, she would cross her legs while I tried to help her with her shoes," Julie said. "It was worth it to hear her giggle."

In just a year, Mary Jean's medications were reduced to minimal doses or eliminated. Her behavior plan was abandoned, and the symptoms of her bipolar with rapid cycling diagnosis diminished to an occasional night of disrupted sleep. She was able to dress herself and help make her bed, keep her room neat, and put away her own clean laundry. She stopped grabbing food from the plates of other people at the table. She ate more slowly, knowing that no one would take her food away from her, as had happened at Belchertown and in group homes.

Mary Jean is now held up as an example of what the shared-living model can accomplish.

Julie's top criterion for accepting Mary Jean into her home — affection — aligns with research by disability experts Robert Bogdan and Steven J. Taylor. They define an accepting relationship between a person with a severe and obvious disability and another person as one that is longstanding and characterized by closeness and affection. In the relationship, they say, the disability is not stigmatizing and the person with the disability is viewed as a full-fledged human being. Julie, David, and their daughters love and value Mary Jean as an affectionate, witty person.

The Morgans' motivation in serving as shared-living providers is personal. When Mary Jean joined them, Julie and David lived with their two daughters, Ashley and Lauren, and two other adults with disabilities. Ashley has since married and moved away. Lauren has intellectual and developmental disabilities.

When Lauren was young, it became clear that she would not be able to live independently as an adult. Julie decided the best way to understand the system of care was to get a job in a group home. She didn't like what she saw, so she and David created what they call their family business — a shared-living home — to provide Lauren with meaningful employment and a safe place to live. Lauren is paid for specific responsibilities in the household that she carries out extremely well. Over time, she became Mary Jean's designated aide and friend.

The Morgans' home is filled with art and laughter. The first time I visited, the smells of modeling clay and poster paint blended with the aroma of a pot of stew. Mary Jean was not yet home from her daytime activities. Every weekday, she leaves the house to spend the morning and early afternoon with a day worker. They take walks through parks and along Onota Lake, participate in neighborhood cleanup programs, and visit residents at a skilled nursing and rehabilitation facility, where Mary Jean claps to the music of sing-alongs. She eats lunch at the worker's home or occasionally goes to a fast-food restaurant or for a picnic.

With Julie and David, service provider and family merged. Dramatic changes began when attention shifted from Mary Jean's deficits to the multiple ways she could communicate. The Morgans watched her body language. They listened to vocalizations, which may or may not sound like words. They were alert for the sign language gestures she's learned. They charted her moods and reactions to the activities of the household and provided options.

When she was out in the community during her first few years with the Morgans, Mary Jean occasionally kicked others or took off her shirt in public places when she became agitated. Julie bought sports bras for Mary Jean to wear every day, thereby ensuring appropriate coverage. As day program staff learned to read her feelings and moods, episodes of aggression and self-abuse decreased and eventually became virtually nonexistent.

Mary Jean still has adjustment periods when the seasons change. The winter holidays especially affect her. She still raises her voice when feeling stressed, but rarely screams. She doesn't pull hair or strip in public.

Mary Jean can choose to be part of the noisy bustle of the kitchen or retreat to the quiet of her own comfortable, soundproofed bedroom. Although the remainder of her teeth were extracted in 2002 and she is unable to wear dentures, Mary Jean eats a wide range of nutritious foods — and treats — that are cut into small pieces or pureed. Most of the time, her behavior is appropriate and sociable. She continues to learn and use more words and signs to make her needs and preferences known.

The Morgans' household is active, with many friends and family coming and going. Mary Jean says hello to everyone in the living area, then says "bye" and goes to her own room when she's had enough. She continues to be upset by loud, unexpected noises, but instead of screaming when nervous or upset, she often asks for a hug.

After three years with the Morgans, Mary Jean's residential assessment said that she was calm, relaxed, and comfortable in her home. She seemed extremely happy, full of smiles and hugs and kisses. She made her own choices regarding how she wants to spend her time, what she would like to eat, when she would like to go out for a ride or walk, and when she wants to go to bed. She enjoyed visits with her brothers and sisters.

Mary Jean appears to have memories of past traumas. Julie recounted a routine doctor's visit when Mary Jean waited calmly in the exam room. But when the nurse started to put sticky leads on her chest for an EKG, Mary Jean screamed "no shock." We surmise that at some point, perhaps at Belchertown, she endured shock treatment. Another time, Julie thought Mary Jean would enjoy a scenic car ride to Shelburne Falls. But Mary Jean freaked after twenty minutes and Julie turned around. Only later did Julie realize that they were following the route Mary Jean would have experienced as a child between Pittsfield and Belchertown.

Julie observed that Mary Jean has many characteristics of autism, including echolalia (repeating back words), sensitivity to sounds, and ritualized behavior. For example, Mary Jean touches two walls, in the same place each time, before she takes a shower. For a while, Mary Jean insisted on opening the refrigerator door the first thing in the morning. Early childhood symptoms — delayed developmental milestones, talking late and then losing the words she'd learned, seizures, refusing to eat — all align with an autism diagnosis. If Mary Jean were a young child today, she'd likely be considered on the autism spectrum with significant developmental and intellectual disabilities. Had the knowledge and resources available now been available to Mary Jean in the early 1960s, she could have avoided decades of abuse and developed more functionally.

Mary Jean and Julie were born on the same day in 1959, Mary Jean in Pittsfield and Julie in England. Through some miracle, they found one another. Julie became the connection that allowed Mary Jean to escape the institution and group home system that failed her so miserably for so many years.

Mary Jean's capacity to connect and show affection grew as she felt safe and secure. Julie has promised Mary Jean she'll be with her forever, and Mary Jean seems to understand that she won't have to move again. When Julie blows a kiss, Mary Jean slaps her own cheek to catch the kiss.

15
RELEASE

I thought my parents' pain would ease as it became clear that Mary Jean was happy and out of harm's way with the Morgans. Instead, they descended into a strange kind of denial. They didn't open letters sent by the state. Required forms went unsigned. Tim handled meetings and phone calls about Mary Jean's care, although legally, my parents remained her guardians.

For five years or so, their health remained good enough to spend each summer at the cottage in Pittsfield, but they'd visit Mary Jean only a few times during their stay. "It disrupts her routine to see us," they'd tell me in our weekly phone calls, or "We planned to visit but didn't feel up to the drive." I felt sad as I listened to their excuses. The Morgans' house was an easy fifteen-minute drive from the cottage. Fear that Mary Jean would act out, despite reports that her negative behaviors had plummeted, kept them away. And seeing Mary Jean thriving in a family home heightened their guilt about sending her to Belchertown and allowing her to live in abusive group homes for so many years.

Both my parents developed serious dementia. Eileen was at their condo in South Carolina every day, bringing groceries, driving them to medical appointments, and doing everything she could to help them live on their own. She arranged for a home health aide, but Papa fired the woman after a single visit because he could not admit that he needed support. When Mom was hospitalized for a hip replacement, Papa wandered around the neighborhood, confused and unable to find his way home. It was clear they were no longer safe at home and they moved to an assisted living facility.

Mom died just before Thanksgiving in 2009. Her wish was to be cremated in South Carolina and her remains buried in Pittsfield. Papa was so frail that we were sure he'd pass away soon after Mom's death. It seemed more practical to wait and have one burial. But he hung on, month after month. Eileen found it terribly distressing to have Mom's ashes in her house. She tucked the urn in her closet, next to her winter boots, so they'd be out of sight until Mom could be properly honored.

Finally, more than a year-and-a-half after Mom's death, my siblings and I gathered in Pittsfield. Papa was far too weak to travel from South Carolina. Julie and Lauren Morgan brought Mary Jean for the brief ceremony held next to the plot that Mom and Papa had purchased on a hilltop in St. Joseph's Cemetery.

In tears, I gently placed on Mom's grave a few tiny whelk and scallop shells she had collected from her beloved Sanibel Island when she lived in Florida. The air chilled and storm clouds rolled over the mountains. I thought about the contrast between the warm sun of a Florida beach and the cold wind of Pittsfield. It seemed a metaphor for the rare moments of peace she found in a life dominated by anguish and guilt.

Eileen, Sharon, Mary Jean, Paul, Tim, and Ann (Tim's wife) —
St. Joseph's Cemetery, Pittsfield, November 2011

Paul, Eileen, Sharon, Julie, Mary Jean, and Tim — Home of
Mary Jean and the Morgan family, Dalton, November 2011

Less than two months after Mom's service, Papa died. We assembled again at St. Joseph's for a burial, and once more, Mary Jean, Julie, and Lauren joined us. This time, Eileen, Paul, and I had an afternoon free to revisit Pittsfield. We drove past our grandparents' house on Circular Avenue, the cottage on Pontoosuc Lake, and the family homes of our childhoods. The house on Peck's Road — the site of Papa's treasured garden and the barn that had been my sanctuary before Papa's rage ruined it — was by then, in a strange coincidence, a group home for intellectually and developmentally disabled adults.

"Let's knock on the door," Paul said, "I'd like to look around."

My breath caught. I wanted to put the past to rest, and I was terrified that the life I'd patched together would collapse if I stepped foot on the property.

"Come on," Paul urged. "It would be cool to see it."

Eileen froze in the passenger seat next to me. She, too, had memories from this house that skulked her dreams.

I pulled the rental car into the driveway and drove slowly up the hill. Paul jumped cheerfully out of the back seat and approached the kitchen door. He was very young when we lived on Peck's Road and had no idea that grim memories haunted Eileen and me. I was still behind the wheel when I realized a jacket-clad arm was beckoning us into the kitchen. Eileen squeezed my hand.

"We can do this," she said.

"I'm heading out to the store," the group home attendant said. "Have a look around. Just shut the door when you leave."

And with that, we were on our own, free to poke around. Eileen went from nook to cranny, remembering the hiding places she used to cope with the chaos around her as a scared little girl — behind the vacuum cleaner in the closet under the stairs, in the butler's pantry off the dining room, beneath the coats in the cedar closet in the basement. Painful emotions accumulated as she walked through the house, and she was sobbing as she approached the coal cellar where Papa had stored potatoes.

Rooms had been reconfigured to meet fire-code requirements for a group home, but the house was surprisingly unchanged. The built-in bookshelf in the bedroom I shared with Paul remained, painted white instead of lime green. In a closet, we spotted patches of the Asian-themed wallpaper that had so impressed Mom when she first saw the house — red birds with green tails, white and yellow flowers that vaguely resembled cherry blossoms. In Tim's bedroom hung the same curtains we had left behind more than forty years earlier.

I felt wobbly as I approached the garage. This was the only way into the barn and hayloft. Eileen put her hand on my elbow, silently urging me to step away. I ignored her and reached for the garage door handle, rusted and half-buried beneath dead leaves. I pulled. The locked door did not move. Relieved, I stepped backwards.

As a very young child, I had learned to bury my feelings, to entomb my memories. Even as an adult, I had gone along with Papa's storylines for many years: Nothing bad happened to me. My parents had no choice — even when they were exposed to the horrors of Belchertown — about keeping Mary Jean there. We were a happy family. Standing by the barn, I realized I could finally look honestly at fifty years of muddled truths and untruths. During one of my last visits with him, Papa held my shoulders and said: "Sharon, I really love you." I stared into his eyes, watching a tear slide down his cheek. I believed him. And yet I felt the anguish of unhealed wounds.

His death was a turning point. For the first time, I recognized a deeply held belief that had ruled my life: Holding onto my pain was necessary to hold him accountable for his abusive actions. With his death, I was able to start down a pathway of release and forgiveness.

The route to healing included a trip to Belchertown the following year. I traveled from Arizona to Massachusetts alone. Almost thirty-five years after Mary Jean had left the institution, I returned to the abandoned grounds in October 2012. My first stop was a place I had not known existed: the school cemetery. For most of its history, Belchertown State School buried residents who died in a wooded area across the highway from the school campus.

Albert Warner, one of the first children admitted to Belchertown School for the Feeble-Minded in 1922, left the school as an adult and often visited the graveyard to pay respect to his state school friends who died. Cement gravestones in the unkempt woods had only the numbers assigned to Belchertown residents upon commitment — not names — underscoring the notion that these people were less than human. But Warner knew where his friends were buried. And when the cemetery became a dumping ground for trash and landscaping debris, he decided to do something.

With his wife, Agnes, also a former resident of the institution, he enlisted the help of friends and Ben Ricci, the force behind the landmark class action. In 1987, the state agreed to erect a memorial with the names of people buried in the graveyard. The site was renamed the Warner Pine Grove Memorial Cemetery in 1994. Stones with the names and dates of those buried replaced the numbered markers. A plaque reads: "The cemetery reflects the changing attitudes towards people with disabilities during this century. Just as this cemetery lay hidden, so too were individuals with mental retardation. As time passed, the cemetery, like the institution, fell into disrepair. Slowly reform came and with this new thinking those once confined took their rightful places in our communities."

The cemetery was well-maintained when I visited in 2012, but most of the school campus was in bad shape. No trespassing signs speckled the property. In contrast to the fierce competition among rural towns to be selected by the state as the site for the new school for the feeble-minded in 1916, local officials struggled to secure redevelopers of the campus after it closed in 1992. Today, a Google search of Belchertown State School turns up websites of ghost-hunters and photographers of abandoned New England buildings.

The sky was gray on the day of my visit, but autumn colors brightened the campus. Red and golden maples complemented maroon boards covering the window openings of red brick buildings. I stared at the four-sided clock towering over the administration building. Dirty white paint peeled below the blue cupola, with clock hands stopped at six-thirty. A short walk along broken pavement brought me to a dormitory. I climbed a metal staircase that seemed reasonably sturdy and peered through an opening in the bricks. Dirty linen rested on foul mattresses. Two decades after the institution had closed, the stink remained.

I moved on, navigating from memory, and found Tadgell Nursery. When Mary Jean had moved there from an older building in the 1960s, my parents hailed the improvement. Yet Judge Tauro's visit to Tadgell in 1973 led to his conclusion that no "expert opinion would convince me that little girls are supposed to drink out of urinals."

A light rain bathed tears from my face as I walked up the moss-covered ramp of the concrete gazebo across the street from Tadgell. I remembered Tim, Eileen, and Paul running up and down the ramp when we were children, as I stood with Mom and Papa on the sidewalk, ever the vigilant oldest sister, holding Mary Jean's hand. The ramp was too steep for her to climb, even with help.

In time, the physical remnants of Belchertown State School will be transformed or bulldozed. Part of the farm acreage is home to a community garden and sub-leased farm parcels. A small part of the campus is used for public schools, teen and senior centers, the town's police station, and an American Legion hall. The town rejected a proposal to construct a prison on the site in the early 1990s. Sundry plans for a resort, an assisted-living facility, apartments, and offices have not come to fruition. But the Belchertown State School Friends Association has been resurrected, and plans are underway for interpretive plaques and a small museum.

Belchertown State School must be commemorated in a way far more significant than the cemetery monument. Plaques and a museum are valuable, but not enough. Instead, we must study the history of Belchertown and its sister institutions throughout the country. We must apply the lessons learned to public policy. It is a tough slog.

16
FRONT BURNER

The rape and unexpected birth at Hacienda HealthCare in Phoenix made the news throughout the country and around the world in the early weeks of 2019. After an intensive investigation, a licensed practical nurse who was responsible for the victim's care during the time of the assault was arrested by Phoenix police. Court records said the suspect's DNA matched the baby's paternal DNA profile.

As the story unfolded, it became clear that this was not simply a "one bad apple" situation. The problems were deep and systemic. A statute passed in 1997 exempted Hacienda from state licensing requirements. Hacienda also had benefited from a state law giving the nonprofit a monopoly on the privately-owned intermediate care market. The *Arizona Republic* quoted a senior policy advisor to Gov. Doug Ducey: "They had all the negotiating power. The state had to pay whatever they were asking, even if it was the highest rate in the country." News media reported that the CEO, who resigned in the wake of the scandal after twenty-eight years at Hacienda, drew a salary and bonuses of more than $600,000 a year. Board members had a long history of nepotism and contracting with Hacienda through their private businesses.

The board chair reaped lucrative commissions by brokering health insurance for about 800 Hacienda employees for decades. Hacienda also owned two for-profit companies that sold medical equipment and provided home health care. Principals of the two for-profits included Hacienda board members.

Hacienda's governing board hired a former county attorney to conduct an internal investigation of patient safety, security, and procedures. He quit after the board failed to cooperate in the investigation. Such a governance failure is unacceptable. The federal government directs billions of dollars of public funding to both for-profit and nonprofit providers of services to individuals with disabilities each year. It is in the interest of taxpayers as well as vulnerable individuals to hold the governing boards of providers accountable for carrying out their oversight duties. Requirements for adherence to governance best practices must be spelled out in government contracts.

The Hacienda victim's family described her as alert but non-verbal, with limited ability to move her head, neck, and limbs. "She has feelings, likes to be read to, enjoys soft music, and is capable of responding to people she is familiar with, especially family," they told the media through their lawyer. "The important thing is that she is a beloved daughter, albeit with significant intellectual disabilities."

That description reminded me of Mary Jean. More than half a century had passed since Mary Jean was institutionalized, yet throughout the United States, we still have not figured out how to keep our most vulnerable kinfolk safe.

Most of Hacienda's revenue came from the government, and the governor and state agencies quickly announced criminal and regulatory investigations. The governor also issued an executive order requiring three state agencies to review protocols and jointly develop training for both care providers and for parents and guardians to help prevent, recognize, and report abuse and neglect of vulnerable people. Among other things, the agencies must ensure that state contracts related to the care of individuals with disabilities include a requirement that potential staff involved in care are checked through the Adult Protective Services Registry before being hired. Finally, the executive order created a task force to recommend improvements.

I felt waves of nausea every time new layers of the story came to light. The connection felt all too close to the abuse Mary Jean had suffered. I remembered Judge Tauro's words in a 1987 interview about the class-action suit in Massachusetts: "No matter how good government is, it runs on a crisis basis. Problems of the retarded were put on the back burner. The lawsuit made it a front-burner problem."

Now, the horrific events at Hacienda HealthCare put the prevention of abuse and neglect on the front burner in Arizona. But I feared that the disbelief and outrage would flare for a few months and then fade away, without the changes in policies, regulations, and laws necessary to truly improve the system of care.

Shocking details about Hacienda continued to emerge. According to a notice of claim filed by the victim's family against the state, there were more than eighty entries in her chart that should have led caregivers to suspect a pregnancy. And in June 2019, state agencies stepped in when maggots were found around the surgical incision of another patient in the Hacienda facility.

When I was asked to facilitate the task force to improve protections for individuals with developmental and other disabilities, most people involved had no idea how close this topic was to my heart. I hadn't been able to help Mary Jean when she was in Belchertown. Now, I had a chance to help drive positive change in Arizona for people like her. I was grateful for the chance to work alongside the family members, individuals with disabilities, advocacy organizations, agency staff, care providers, and legislators on the task force to craft solutions.

The first steps toward change came in Spring 2019 when the state legislature passed bills to require licensure of all intermediate care facilities by the state health department, and expanded background checks, training standards for assisted living caregivers, and mandatory reporting of suspected abuse, neglect, and exploitation. A bill also was signed to allow electronic monitoring in the common areas of group homes and care facilities.

Good people with passion and commitment are advocating on behalf of people with intellectual and developmental disabilities. But Dorothea Dix and Samuel Howe in the 19th century and the community-based care advocates in the 20th century had passion and commitment, too. And here we are.

17

REFORMING THE SYSTEM

After so many decades of being a part of Mary Jean's suffering, my siblings and I are comforted that she is safe and happy with the Morgans. The *Ricci* consent decree entitles her to a higher level of public funding than is available to the majority of people with developmental and intellectual disabilities. Unlike most of her peers throughout the country, she will have adequate funding and court-guaranteed access to all necessary services for the rest of her life.

Yet even with *Ricci* status, Mary Jean suffered decades of sub-par care in group and shared-living facilities after she left Belchertown. She is thriving mostly thanks to the Morgans' unusual motivation for creating a shared-living home and their remarkable personalities and commitment. Unfortunately, their vision and dedication are not easily replicated.

The abuse and neglect Mary Jean experienced for so many years underscore the need for a public policy commitment to caring for people with intellectual and developmental disabilities. Progress is uneven and too often moves backward. The shift during the 1970s and '80s from institutions to community-based care has not been a panacea. Social workers throughout the country carry heavy caseloads; staff in group homes and care facilities are underpaid and often inadequately trained; too many shared-living providers are motivated by a paycheck. Stories of neglect and abuse abound. Unbelievable as it seems, some people are calling for a move away from community-based care and back to an institutional model.

The issue is complex, and solutions are not straightforward. More than 7 million people with intellectual disabilities live in the United States today and their needs are many and varied: primary health care, habilitative and rehabilitative services and devices, durable medical equipment, mental health and behavioral services, chronic disease management, and dental, vision, and geriatric care. Achieving and maintaining good health depends on a legion of providers trained to meet specific needs: primary care physicians, nurse-practitioners, and physician assistants; physical and occupational therapists; orthopedists; psychologists and psychiatrists; social workers; dentists and orthodontists; and specialists such as cardiologists, gastroenterologists, geriatricians, and ophthalmologists.

Beyond health care, their well-being requires that they be welcomed and integrated into our communities. They need wraparound coordination of comprehensive services. They need safe homes. And they need strong legal and educational protections against neglect and abuse.

Vulnerable individuals, their loved ones, and their caregivers must be clear that abuse arises from a cruel exertion of power and control. Rates of sexual assault are far higher for people with disabilities than the general population. People with a wide range of cognitive abilities can learn ways to recognize danger and seek help. Education about boundaries, healthy sexual expression, and safety should be widely available. This is especially important when a caregiver's help is needed for hygiene, getting dressed, medical care, and so forth. The vulnerable person needs to be clear about the difference between appropriate touching and abusive behaviors.

Families need support, too. My parents believed they had no choice when they institutionalized Mary Jean in 1962. Doctors and clergy said that sending Mary Jean to Belchertown was the best thing for the rest of our family, yet my parents' anger and guilt wreaked havoc in all of our lives. Our story is not unique; millions of families continue to struggle to find safe, compassionate care for their loved ones. And the problem is growing as people with disabilities live longer and their family members age and pass away.

Sharon and Mary Jean—
Home of Mary Jean and the Morgan family, Dalton, 2017

What will it take to ensure that tragedies like Belchertown and horrifying incidents like the rape at Hacienda are not repeated?

An essential first step is casting off the vestiges of segregation demanded a century ago by those who believed the "feeble-minded" should be quarantined. I grew up hearing the jeers "retard" and "moron" on streets and playgrounds. Anti-bullying campaigns and legislation like Rosa's Law, which removed the term mental retardation from the federal lexicon, have not stopped the mocking and marginalization of people who are different. Indeed, I wonder how long the expression "intellectual disability" will be in favor. As *New York Times* columnist Dan Barry mused: "The question now is whether 'intellectual disability' will remain the preference, or, like its predecessors, devolve into a derogatory taunt. The answer seems to hinge on society's ability to shed its prejudices and move past that stigmatizing sense of otherness."

Mary Jean — Home of Mary Jean and the Morgan family, Dalton, 2017

Caring for people with intellectual, developmental, and other disabilities is a social responsibility we all share. We must reform — re-form — our system of care. How we care for vulnerable people is rooted in our values as a society. A federal judge said in 1973 that little girls should not be drinking from urinals; it is unacceptable that decades later, neglect and abuse are widespread throughout the country. Reimbursement decreases after the Great Recession resulted in serious workforce recruiting and retention problems, inadequate training, and decreased supervision of direct-service staff.

Creating a new system will take progressive public policies and money. Solutions will arise from partnerships among nonprofit organizations, state agencies, and the federal government. There are promising models of care scattered throughout the country, but for the most part, they require financial resources many families lack. We must identify and fund the models that work best in reducing isolation, promoting respect, and delivering high-quality services. In many cases, this means home-based services even for people who are medically fragile, such as those who use ventilators to breathe.

Group homes and facilities must be well-regulated and staffed with well-trained, well-supervised, and well-compensated professionals who provide care that's matched to the needs of each individual. The Arizona Association of Providers for People with Disabilities, like scores of advocates across the country, is calling for a funding increase to pay caregivers more than the minimum wage.

We must incentivize and expand workforce education and training to ensure that positions are staffed by compassionate people who know what they're doing. We must vote for legislators who are willing to appropriate the dollars needed to be a responsible and respectful society. This might be the most difficult thing of all. As Jon Meyers, executive director of The Arc of Arizona, said: "No one was ever voted into or out of office as a result of the care for people with developmental disabilities." It's time to tell our legislators, "This is an issue that *will* change my vote!"

In 1950, Pearl S. Buck shared a fundamental truth she learned from her daughter: ". . . all people are equal in their humanity and all have the same human rights. None is to be considered less, as a human being, than any other, and each must be given his place and safety in the world."

She wrote that other parents often asked her how they could bear the sorrow of having child who does not grow mentally. She responded: "Only to endure is not enough. Endurance can be a harsh and bitter root in one's life, bearing poisonous and gloomy fruit, destroying other lives. Endurance is only the beginning. There must be acceptance and the knowledge that sorrow fully accepted brings its own gifts. For there is an alchemy to sorrow. It can be transmuted into wisdom, which, if it does not bring joy, can yet bring happiness."

Without a doubt, Mary Jean's anguish cut deeply into the hearts of everyone in our family, starting with the seizures, the days and nights of screaming when she was at home, and continuing through the decades of abuse and self-abuse at Belchertown. After she returned to Berkshire County and community-based care, it went on with more abuse, overmedication, and hospitalizations.

As a small child, I became hard-wired to believe that if something could go terribly wrong, it surely will. When I was seven, guilt swallowed me after hearing the pediatrician say Mary Jean must go to Belchertown because she could not survive in a family of smart children — and I knew that I was smart. But I was not smart enough to fix her, and neither were my desperate, flailing parents, so despair set in, too.

After many decades, the aching pain has slowly given way to forgiving my parents and myself. I came to understand that every person on this earth — even, to my surprise, me — has worth, not because of what we do or produce, but because we are human. Mary Jean's will to survive, her resilience, and her journey toward happiness have shaped my life. I watched her lash out like the furies of hell at the chaos of unsafe houses and unkind caretakers. Equally powerful is the peace she's found in a stable, dependable home and consistent routines.

Life is full of experiences we don't anticipate. Some are welcomed and thrilling; others are explosive and destructive. From Mary Jean, I learned that a foundation hewn of safety, humor, and love gets all of us through the dark times and the delights.

The artist Marc Chagall said, "If all life moves inevitably toward its end, then we must, during our own, color it with our colors of love and hope."

Mary Jean has gifted all who know her with a brilliant palette.

ACKNOWLEDGMENTS

I offer heartfelt thanks to —

First and foremost, Mary Jean, a sister with dazzling humor and resilience.

Tim, Eileen, and Paul, siblings and cherished lifelong companions.

My parents Jean and Paul, who lived and loved and sought forgiveness as best they could.

My beloved husband Peter, children Katherine and Justin, and grandchildren Johnny and Chiara. You are my inspiration and strength.

The Morgan Family for embracing Mary Jean.

The Collaborative Sparks circle of friends — Maren Showkeir, who is also my editor extraordinaire; Jamie Showkeir, who departed this life far too soon; Regina Blakely; Jennifer Barnes; Robin Postel; Christine Whitney Sanchez; and Reuben Sanchez.

Committed and brilliant activists and early readers of this book — Diedra Freedman and Joyce Millard Hoie.

The many change agents convened by the Arizona Governor's Office to serve on the Abuse & Neglect Prevention Task Force and the Autism Spectrum Disorder Advisory Committee of the Arizona Health Care Cost Containment System.

Guides on my writing journey — Tania Katan, Andrea Avery, Margaret Rode, Robert Hornick, Christina Baldwin, Ann Linnea, and Sharon Blackie.

Loyal friends for decades — Arlene Lalouette and Sandra Leal.

Wise counselors — Donna Hawxhurst and the late Sue Morrow.

And I am grateful beyond words for the countless others who have supported me on this journey.

ENDNOTES

A Note on Terminology

What you call people is how you treat them. . . . *"Remarks by the President at the Signing of the 21ˢᵗ Century Communications Act of 2010," 2010, no page number.*

Less than a decade ago, President Barack Obama signed legislation . . . *"Remarks by the President at the Signing of the 21ˢᵗ Century Communications Act of 2010," 2010, no page number.*

Today, the U.S. National Institute of Health describes . . . *"Intellectual and Developmental Disabilities," 2016, no page number.*

Chapter 4

But in 1950 the acclaimed author Pearl S. Buck . . . *Buck, Ladies Home Journal, 35.*

The novelist James Michener . . . *Buck, The Child Who Never Grew, vii.*

The revelation . . . *Buck, The Child Who Never Grew, viii.*

And she experienced depression . . . *Buck, Ladies Home Journal, 154.*

There was no more joy . . . *Buck, Ladies Home Journal, 154.*

Pearl wrote: "Of that month . . . *Buck, Ladies Home Journal, 163.*

The tragedy of mental retardation . . . *Levinson, 25, 42.*

It may be better all around . . . *Spock, 502.*
If the family can afford . . . *Spock, 502-3.*
Wise men and women . . . *Buck, Ladies Home Journal, 146.*

CHAPTER 6

Dorothea Dix, a Boston school teacher . . . *Scheerenberger, 104.*
Howe decried "permanent life asylums . . . *LaBrecque, 17.*
Binet wrote, "We must protest . . . *Scheerenberger, 143.*
The next year, a newspaper article . . . *Hornick, 4.*
He made the case . . . *Fernald, 175.*
Fernald argued that. . . *Fernald, 177.*
The panel made more than 100 . . . *Kennedy, 1963.*
This was the first time . . . *Gettings, 15-16.*
At a ceremony to celebrate . . . *Kennedy, 1963.*

CHAPTER 7

The commission's investigators . . . *Hornick, 86.*
After his death in 1988 . . . *"George Porter, 65, Dies . . . ," B2.*
Dr. Porter helped set up . . . *"BCARC memorializes . . ., " B4.*
He had the opportunity . . . *BCArc, no page number.*
In 1973, the group changed its name . . . *"History of The Arc,"*
     2018, no page number.
There is a hell on earth . . . *Blatt, v-vi.*
Blatt described the fetid odor. . . *Blatt, 22.*
Blatt reported that one attendant . . . *Blatt, 13.*
There is a shame in America. . . . *Blatt, 109.*
We now have a deep sorrow . . . *Blatt, vi.*

CHAPTER 9

On the first page, Park wrote . . . *Park, 3.*
Out of nowhere . . . *Park, 4.*
The Parks concluded . . . *Park, 30.*
The siege that gave . . . *Park, 12.*

When describing the challenges . . . *Park, 33.*
The Siege concluded . . . *Park, 257-8*

CHAPTER 10

Lying in that bed . . . *Sienkiewicz-Mercer, 40.*
She wrote, "At Belchertown the attendants . . . *Sienkiewicz-Mercer, 41.*
When she was finally taken . . . *Sienkiewicz-Mercer, 44.*
She said the ward . . . *Sienkiewicz-Mercer, 49.*
Ruth described a girl . . . *Sienkiewicz-Mercer, 50.*
The state Assistant Commissioner . . . *Fraenkel, Exhibit B.*
Shanks quoted Dr. Philip Wakstein . . . *Shanks, March 17, 1970, 1.*
There is a large room . . . *Shanks, March 17, 1970, 4.*
There is one basic principle . . . *Shanks, March 15, 1970, 24.*
Belchertown was lacking the reforms . . . *Shanks, March 15, 1970, 24.*

CHAPTER 11

In his book, he wrote . . . *Ricci, 5-6*
After a year of visits . . . *Hornick, 91.*
Commissioner Dr. Milton Greenblatt . . . *Hornick, 92.*
A significant proportion of the . . . *Gettings, 67.*
After discussion . . . *Ricci, 96-97.*
I never knew such things . . . *Belin, 55.*
In an eerie echo . . . *Klein, 8.*
Another parent . . . *Klein, 1.*
It is a nightmare of a system . . . *Klein, 8.*
Klein concluded . . . *Klein, 1, 3.*

CHAPTER 12

He asked his law clerk . . . *Belin, 56-7.*
The case collapsed . . . *Belin, 58-60.*
To find the facts . . . *Belin, 60.*

CHAPTER 13

An article in *The Springfield Morning Union* . . . *Saenger, 22A.*
A 1985 article . . . *Moore, 6.*
The Department . . . *Advocacy Network News, no page number.*
Mary Jean pulled a lady's hair . . . *Morton, no page number.*
And she decried . . . *Morton, no page number.*

CHAPTER 14

Julie's top criterion . . . *Bogdan, 278.*

CHAPTER 16

The *Arizona Republic* quoted a senior policy advisor . . . *Innes, "Hacienda HealthCare...," 2019.*
Board members had a long history . . . *McCambridge, 2019.*
Principals of the two for-profits . . . *Bizapedia, 2019.*
The Hacienda victim's family . . . *D'Anna, 2019.*
I remembered Judge Tauro's . . . *Massachusetts Gaining ..., 1987, Section 1, 30.*

CHAPTER 17

As *New York Times* columnist . . . *Barry, SR6.*
The Arizona Association of Providers . . . *Silverman, 2019, no page number.*
As Jon Meyers, executive director . . . *Silverman, 2019, no page number.*
In 1950, Pearl S. Buck shared . . . *Buck, Ladies Home Journal, 164.*
Only to endure . . . *Buck, Ladies Home Journal, 35.*
The artist Marc Chagall . . . *Chagall, Merritt Gallery, no page number.*

SOURCES CONSULTED

"About BCArc." Information from Berkshire County Arc, 2019.

Advocacy Network News. Amherst, MA: March 1996.

Anglen, Robert. "Rape at Health-care Facility Reveals Questionable Deals, Nepotism by Board Leaders." *Arizona Republic*, February 19, 2019.

Anglen, Robert, and Stephanie Innes, "Patient Rape Case: Investigator Quits, Says Hacienda Board Stymied Him." *Arizona Republic*, March 1, 2019.

Azzopardi, Rich. "Health Aide Pleads Guilty to Assault." *The Berkshire Eagle*, March 14, 2004, B2.

Barry, Dan. "Giving a Name, and Dignity, to a Disability." *The New York Times*, May 7, 2016.

"BCARC Memorializes Dr. George Porter." *The Berkshire Eagle*, December 6, 1988, B4.

Belin, Richard d'A. *Benchmarks XXIV: The Life and Legacy of Joseph L. Tauro.* Boston: Massachusetts Continuing Legal Education, Inc., 2011.

Bizapedia. "Innovative Home Health Care, Inc." updated April 13, 2016 and "South Mountain Home Supply, Inc.," updated April 17, 2016.

Blatt, Burton, and Fred Kaplan. *Christmas in Purgatory: A Photographic Essay on Mental Retardation.* Boston: Allyn & Bacon, 1966. Rev. ed. Syracuse, NY: Human Policy Press, 1974.

Bodgon, Robert, and Steven J. Taylor. "The Social Construction of Humanness: Relationships with Severely Disabled People." Chap. 13 in *Interpreting Disability: A Qualitative Reader*, edited by Philip M. Ferguson, Dianne L. Ferguson, and Steven J. Taylor. New York: Teachers College Press, 1992.

Buck, Pearl S. "The Child Who Never Grew." *Ladies Home Journal*, 35, 146-50, 152, 154, 156, 159-60, 163-65, 167, 169, 171, May 1950.

— — — . *The Child Who Never Grew*. Foreword by James. A Michener. 2nd ed. Rockville, MD: Woodbine House, 1992.

Burkitt, Bree. "'We Had No Idea This Patient Was Pregnant': Nurse's 911 Call Details Surprise Birth at Hacienda Facility." *Arizona Republic*, January 11, 2019.

Chagall, Marc. Quoted by Merritt Gallery, Baltimore, MD.

D'Anna, John. "Hacienda Rape Victim Is Not Comatose, Lawyer Representing Her Family Says." *Arizona Republic*, January 18, 2019.

Dix, Dorothea L. "Memorial To The Legislature of Massachusetts, 1843" in *The History of Mental Retardation, Collected Papers, Vol. I*, 3-30, edited by Marvin Rosen, Gerald R. Clark, and Marvin S. Kivitz. Baltimore: University Park Press, 1976.

Ducey, Douglas A. "Letter to Arizona Attorney General Mark Brnovich." Unpublished, February 5, 2019.

Dybwad, Gunnar. "Are We Retarding the Retarded?" Friends of the Samuel Gridley Howe Library and the Dybwad Family: October 1960.

Fernald, Walter E. "The Burden of Feeble-Mindedness, Appendix H, Annual Discourse, Delivered June 12, 1912." Reproduced in *Report on the Care and Control of the Defective and Feeble-minded in Ontario*, by Frank Egerton Hodgins, Legislative Assembly of Ontario. Toronto: A.T. Wilgress, 1919, 175-178.

Fraenkel, William A. *A Twenty-Four Hour Visit to a State School for the Mentally Retarded*. February 14, 1969. Reproduced as Exhibit B, Massachusetts General Court, *Report of the Joint Special Commission on Belchertown State School and Monson State Hospital*, March 14, 1971.

"George Porter, 65, Dies, City Pediatrician 35 Years." *The Berkshire Eagle*, January 9, 1988, B2.

Gettings, Robert M. *Forging a Federal-State Partnership: A History of Federal Developmental Disabilities Policy*. Washington, DC: American Association on Intellectual and Developmental Disabilities and Alexandria, VA: The National Association of State Directors of Developmental Disabilities Services, 2011.

Herr, Stanley S. *Rights and Advocacy for Retarded People*. Lexington, MA: D.C. Heath and Co., 1983.

"History Notes, 1966." Massachusetts Department of Mental Health, Social Networks and Archival Context Archival Collection.

"History of The Arc." Information from The Arc, 2019.

Hornick, Robert. *The Girls and Boys of Belchertown: A Social History of the Belchertown State School for the Feeble-Minded*. Amherst: University of Massachusetts Press, 2012.

Howe, S. G. *Letters and Journals of Samuel Gridley Howe*. Boston: Dana Estes & Co., 1909. Conway, MA: Disability History Museum.

Howe, S.G. *Report Made to the Legislature of Massachusetts, Upon Idiocy*. Boston: Coolidge & Wiley, 1848. Reproduced in *Medicine & Society in America*. New York: Arno Press and The New York Times, 1972.

Innes, Stephanie. "'Anything Could Happen': Parents of Hacienda HealthCare Patients Disagree on Quality of Care." *Arizona Republic*, February 12, 2019.

——— ."Arizona Pushes Back Against Hacienda Closure, Gives Company Ultimatum," *Arizona Republic*, February 8, 2019.

——— . "Hacienda HealthCare has a History of Special Protection from State. *Arizona Republic*, January 28, 2019.

"Intellectual and Developmental Disabilities." *National Institutes of Health, U.S. Department of Health and Human Services*, June 30, 2018.

J.G.W. "Instruction of Idiots." *Friends' Review*, 1849. Conway, MA: Disability History Museum.

"John F. Kennedy and People with Intellectual Disabilities." John F. Kennedy Presidential Library and Museum, University of Massachusetts, Boston.

Klein, Joe. "Belchertown: Budget Cuts Kill Kids." *Real Paper* [Boston], December 20, 1972, 1, 5, 8.

Kugel, Robert B., and Wolf Wolfensberger, eds. *Changing Patterns in Residential Services for the Mentally Retarded.* Washington, DC: President's Committee on Mental Retardation, January 10, 1969. Conway, MA: Disability History Museum.

LaBrecque, Donald. *A Historical Perspective on the Lives of People Labeled with an Intellectual Disability in Massachusetts.* Learning and Development, Central/West Regional Office, Department of Developmental Services, 2002.

Levinson, Abraham. *The Mentally Retarded Child.* Westport, CT: Greenwood Press, 1965, revised 1978.

"Massachusetts Gaining in its Care for Retarded." *New York Times,* January 4, 1987.

McCambridge, Ruth. "Can the Rape at Hacienda HealthCare Be Laid at the Feet of the Board?" *Nonprofit Quarterly,* March 6, 2019.

Moore, Steve. "A Home Near Home: Retarded Citizens Return to the Community." *Berkshire Sampler, The Berkshire Eagle,* August 25, 1985, 6-8.

Morton, Manzell. Unpublished correspondence to the Commissioner of the Massachusetts Department of Mental Retardation, January 14, 2003.

Náñez, Dianna M. "Doctor Who Cared for Hacienda HealthCare Rape Victim Has Been Suspended, Another Resigns." *Arizona Republic,* January 21, 2019.

Nirje, Bengt. "The Normalization Principle and Its Human Management Implications." *Changing Patterns in Residential Services for the Mentally Retarded.* Washington, DC: President's Committee on Mental Retardation, January 10, 1969. Conway, MA: Disability History Museum.

Noll, Steven and James W. Trent, Jr. *Mental Retardation in America: A Historical Reader.* New York: New York University Press, 2004.

Oettinger, Katherine B., "Opening Doors for the Retarded Child," *New York Times Magazine,* May 12, 1963, 68-9.

Orzechowski, Ed. *You'll like it here. The Story of Donald Vitkus Belchertown Patient #3394*. Amherst, MA: Levellers Press, 2016.

Park, Clara Claiborne. *The Siege: A Family's Journey into the World of an Autistic Child*. Boston: Back Bay Books, 1982.

"Public Law 111–256." Washington, DC: U.S. Government Publishing Office, October. 5, 2010, 2643-5.

"Remarks by the President at the Signing of the 21st Century Communications Act of 2010." White House Archives, October 8, 2010.

Ricci, Benjamin. *Crimes Against Humanity: A Historical Perspective*. New York: iUniverse, 2004.

Rosen, Marvin, Gerald R. Clark, and Marvin S. Krivitz. *The History of Mental Retardation: Collected Papers, Volumes 1 & 2*. Baltimore: University Park Press, 1976.

Saenger, Peter. "Friends Picket Friends at Belchertown School." *The Morning Union* [Springfield, MA], June 22, 1976, 22A.

Scheerenberger, R.C. *A History of Mental Retardation*. Baltimore: Paul H. Brookes Publishing, 1983.

Schworm, Peter. "Groundbreaking Federal Judge to Step Back." *Boston Globe*, August 15, 2013.

Schwartzapfel, Beth. "The Judge." *Brown Alumni Magazine*. January/February 2015.

Scott, Esther. "Judge Tauro and the Care of the Retarded in Massachusetts." Case Study #C15-87-739.0, Kennedy School of Government, Harvard University, 1987.

Shanks, James M. "The Tragedy of Belchertown." *Springfield Republican* and *Springfield Union* [MA], March 15-20, 1970.

Sienkiewicz-Mercer, Ruth, and Steven B. Kaplan. *I Raise My Eyes to Say Yes: A Memoir*. Boston: Houghton Mifflin, 1989.

Silverman, Amy. "'It Could Be Any of Us': Arizona Patient's Sexual Assault Reveals Lack of Protection." *The Guardian*, February 3, 2019.

Spock, Benjamin. *The Common Sense Book of Baby and Child Care*. New York: Duell, Sloan and Pearce, 1946.

Stirling, Nora. *Pearl Buck: A Woman in Conflict*. Piscataway, NJ: New Century, 1983.

Taylor, Steven J. *A Working Paper on the Nature of Life and Experience of Institutionalization at Belchertown State School.* Unpublished. Syracuse University Center on Human Policy, 1975.

———. "Christmas in Purgatory: A Retrospective Look." *Mental Retardation.* Vol. 44, No. 2: 145-9, April 2006.

"They Need Love, They Get Angry, They Bleed." Executive Producer Richard Ahles. Narration by John Sablon and Brad Davis. WITC-TV Channel 3, Hartford, CT. First broadcast January 1973.

Trent, James W., Jr. *Inventing the Feeble Mind: A History of Mental Retardation in the United States.* Berkeley: University of California Press, 1994.

Wolfensberger, Wolf. "The Origin and Nature of Our Institutional Models." *Changing Patterns in Residential Services for the Mentally Retarded.* Washington, DC: President's Committee on Mental Retardation, January 10, 1969. Conway, MA: Disability History Museum.

ABOUT THE AUTHOR

Sharon Flanagan-Hyde was shaped by her experiences as the sister of a resilient woman with significant intellectual and developmental disabilities. Sharon's mainstay is her family: husband, children, grandchildren, and siblings. As a consultant for more than 30 years, Sharon guided nonprofits, healthcare organizations, and government agencies in collaborative initiatives to build strong communities. She is known for bringing out the best in diverse leaders focused on solving complex issues. Sharon is a graduate of Williams College and holds a master's in organizational change from Prescott College. She is committed to ensuring that all vulnerable people are embraced by their communities with compassion and respect.

Contact Sharon through www.flanagan-hyde.com

Made in the USA
San Bernardino, CA
18 February 2020

64632026R00127